LOVE CASTS OUT
FEAR

LOVE CASTS OUT
FEAR

A JIHAD SURVIVOR'S JOURNEY
FROM REVENGE TO REDEMPTION

BROTHER NATHAN

WITH DAVID CULROSS

BakerBooks

a division of Baker Publishing Group
Grand Rapids, Michigan

© 2015 by Brother Nathan

Published by Baker Books
a division of Baker Publishing Group
P.O. Box 6287, Grand Rapids, MI 49516-6287
www.bakerbooks.com

Printed in the United States of America

Library of Congress Cataloging-in-Publication Data
Nathan, Brother, 1955–
    Love casts out fear : a jihad survivor's journey from revenge to
redemption / Brother Nathan with David Culross.
    pages cm
    ISBN 978-0-8010-1688-2 (pbk.)
    1. Nathan, Brother, 1955– 2. Christian biography—Egypt.
3. Egypt—Church history—21st century. I. Culross, David. II. Title.
BR1725.N335A3 2015
276.2′082092—dc23   2015014073
[B]

15 16 17 18 19 20 21   7 6 5 4 3

I would like to dedicate this book to my family. As you read my story, you will understand why.

To my father: in six short years Baba taught me how to live, then he taught me how to die. "For me, to live is Christ and to die is gain" (Phil. 1:21).

To my mother: for more than eighty years Mama has shown us how to trust God . . . for everything. "My God will meet all your needs according to the riches of his glory in Christ Jesus" (Phil. 4:19).

To my wife, Susan: for the past twenty-five years we have walked hand in hand along the path where God has led us. "A wife of noble character . . . is worth far more than rubies. . . . She speaks with wisdom, and . . . her husband . . . praises her (Prov. 31:10, 26, 28).

To my three children, Maggie, Martin, and Michael: you have filled our home with joy and laughter while modeling the love of Jesus. "Your children will be like olive shoots around your table. Yes, this will be the blessing for the man who fears the LORD" (Ps. 128:3–4).

To my brothers and sisters: there is Magdy, who started the ministry . . . and then Onsey, who never knew his Baba . . . and finally Hoda, Phoebe, and Sawsan. From Asyut to Karya Maghola to Cairo, we made the journey together. "Brothers [and sisters] are born for a time of adversity" (Prov. 17:17).

There is no fear in love; but perfect love casteth out fear.

1 John 4:18 KJV

CONTENTS

INTRODUCTION

I first met Brother Nathan in the mid-1990s, then heard him speak at a conference in Jerusalem. He was one of several Christian leaders from around the world who were involved in reaching their own people with the message of Jesus Christ.

One evening we were taken by bus from our hotel to another site, then secluded in a room with absolute security. For the next hour we listened as Nathan described the horrific events that had changed his life forever. As we prepared to leave that evening, we were urged not to share his story publicly, for fear of compromising his safety.

Now Nathan believes it is time for you to hear that story. It is typical of what is happening every day to believers all across the Middle East. I have disguised some names and other distinguishing elements to protect Nathan and other Christians in this part of the world, but the actual scenes are portrayed in authentic, true-to-life detail.

Recently I traveled to many of the places where these events took place. Along the way I discovered that, in spite of Christianity's first-century arrival in Egypt, Islam has been that country's dominant religion for centuries. Today over eighty million Muslims comprise nearly 95 percent of the population, and since 1980 Islam has been the official national religion. The number of Christians from all denominations is less than three million, but this still represents the largest Christian community in any Middle Eastern or North African country. The majority of the country's evangelical believers are found in southern Egypt, where Nathan once lived.

Now I invite you to travel with me to a tiny village in Upper Egypt called Karya Maghola (Kar-EE-ah Mah-GO-lah). You will not find it on a map, but it is still there. The name we have given this town is adapted from an Arabic word that means "any place" or "unknown place." That's because it is just like countless other villages scattered all across this ancient part of the world, where the people and the culture have hardly changed for centuries.

As we become unseen guests walking its winding streets, my hope is that you will begin to see, through Nathan's eyes, how a loving God protects and provides for his children, even in the face of persecution. Then, through the living example of this twenty-first-century disciple, I hope you will catch a glimpse of how our mighty God can do extraordinary things through the lives of ordinary people who fully surrender to his will. Ordinary people like you and like me. Ordinary people just like Brother Nathan.

David Culross

AUTHOR'S NOTE

The story you are about to read chronicles the life of a small boy who became a man in a place that is much in the news these days: the country of Egypt. It tells how one horrific event in his childhood filled him with hatred and a passion for revenge, and how God used that tragedy to teach him the true meaning of forgiveness. You may wonder: Did these things actually happen? Is this story really true? Let me assure you, everything you read here is true. How do I know? Because it is my story.

The chain of events that combine to tell my story began over fifty years ago. Most of the account is based on personal memories that continue to haunt me today. The rest is woven together from firsthand recollections from my mother and other family members and friends who have played a part in this real-life drama. And my story is still being written in these same remote villages of Upper Egypt.

Throughout the book I have made every effort to portray these events exactly as they took place. My prayer is that, somewhere within these pages, God will challenge you to let him direct your path, just as he has directed mine.

Brother Nathan

1

BLACK FRIDAY

The distant crowing of a neighbor's rooster told me that a new day was dawning in the village of Karya Maghola. It was an ordinary little town, no different than countless others scattered across the arid Egyptian landscape. The dark gray of another morning slowly turned to purple, then brightened to orange as the sun pushed its way up from behind the distant mountains. Overhead, tiny black dots of scavenger vultures—often called Pharaoh's chickens—started tracing lazy circles in the sky as they surveyed the parched landscape for food. In many ways, they were much like the people below, who were slowly waking up to another dry and dreary day in the place I once called home.

As daylight began to peek through the window, I rolled over on my sleeping mat and tried to go back to sleep. But it was no use. It was already getting hot in my room as the warm glow of sunrise continued to chase away the shadows from Dark Mountain. People in the village said Dark Mountain was evil, and when I asked why they said lots of bad people lived there. But on that morning its foreboding frown slowly faded as the sky turned blue and the blazing desert sun reached down to bake the dusty streets. It was *always* dusty in Karya Maghola.

Soon the rooster's strident cry was joined by other morning sounds. I heard the bleating voice of my goat calling out to be milked. Next door, Ibrahim was opening his tiny grocery shop, and I could hear the shuffle of sandaled feet as people scurried along the narrow, winding street. The chug-chug-chug of a dilapidated old bus signaled its daily trip to the distant city of Asyut. A smile spread across my face as I remembered it was my favorite day: Friday. *No school today!* I thought. *We will have children's church with Baba.* Fridays were *always* special in Karya Maghola.

My daydreams were abruptly interrupted by Baba's booming voice from the next room. "Time to get up, Nathan!" he called. I threw off my faded sheet, yawned, and stretched as I rubbed the sleep from my eyes. Then I rolled up my lumpy pallet and pulled on my faded *galabayya*, a traditional robe-like garment worn in the Nile Valley region. In the next room Mama was fixing our Friday breakfast of bread, cheese, and goat's milk, a welcome change from the usual meal of beans. And best of all, our family always ate breakfast together on Fridays. But first there were chores for everyone, even a six-year-old boy. I had to visit the rooftop "patio" to care for my goat and gather eggs from the chicken pens. Maybe there would be one or two extras today, so Mama could bake us a special treat.

When the family finally gathered for breakfast, we began with a prayer by Baba. I loved to hear my father pray. It always seemed like God was Baba's very best friend, and he was sitting right there in the same room with us. We ate our simple meal together, all seated on the floor around a low wooden table. As I drank my mug of milk, I thought, *Someday I will be able to pray just like Baba.* After we finished eating, my older sisters helped Mama clear away the dishes. Now the fun could begin. It was time for children's church.

Baba was known in our village as Pastor Latif. Although he had grown up in a poor family, he had studied to be a schoolteacher. It was not long, though, before Baba felt God calling him to leave the teaching profession to become a pastor. So he moved his young family from the tiny village of Shotb to the nearby city of Asyut, where he enrolled in Bible school. He completed his four-year program in only three years while also pastoring his first church, which was close to the school. When he graduated in May 1956, I was only six months old.

Over the next six years Baba ministered in three villages in that same Upper Egypt region. When he became pastor of the church in Karya Maghola, he also assumed the unofficial role of village leader. Because of this, he never needed to make an appointment to visit a family. He would simply knock on their door and they would invite him in. Soon I was tagging along on these visits as if I were my father's little shadow. I would simply say to Mama, "I have to go with Baba."

The life of a village pastor in Upper Egypt was not easy. Baba's salary was very modest, and often he was paid in more practical ways, such as with gifts of food, clothing, or other necessities. With no other staff to help him, Baba was truly the pastor of all the people, including the boys and girls. Our Friday children's service was one that he looked forward to each week. Ministering to boys and girls was almost like being back in the classroom.

Our family's house was built on three levels, which was somewhat different from other houses in the village. There was a rooftop level, with pens for our goat and a few chickens. It also had a simple wood-fired oven, where each Saturday Mama baked our bread. My whole family—two parents and six growing children—lived in four small rooms on the second floor. The furniture was quite basic: several chairs, a bed for my parents, a low table for meals, and a table and benches in the sitting room for anyone who came to visit. If there were overnight guests, the benches could be pushed together to form additional beds.

The ground floor of our house was entirely taken up by the village church. It contained one large room furnished with a small pulpit and a simple table from which Baba served the Lord's Supper. When Baba and I walked downstairs for children's church that Friday, he took along his sturdy, hand-carved walking staff. As was the custom in those days, most village men usually carried one wherever they went, whether they needed it or not.

The church was especially hot and muggy that day, and soon it was jammed with nearly one hundred energetic boys and girls. We spent the next two hours singing happy songs, reciting Bible verses, and learning lessons from God's Word. The morning session ended with all of us gathered around Baba for a Bible story. Then we went running outside for a free time of play. Two of our favorite games were hide-and-seek and racing to the date grove to gather seeds from fallen fruit. The one who captured the most pits was the winner.

When the midday heat became unbearable, we went back inside for a closing prayer. As the boys and girls were heading home, Ibrahim walked over from his shop next door, along with another neighbor named Youssef. Both men were elders in the church, and they needed to talk to Baba about some business matters. They retreated to the shade in front of the church building to escape the blistering rays of the sun. I was right beside my father, as usual.

Suddenly two men in long, dark *galabayyas* came charging down the street. They also wore checkered headdresses called *keffiyehs*, and their faces were covered by scarves. Without uttering a word they pulled out big guns and began shooting at us. The explosive sounds of gunfire echoed through the streets and panic flooded me. I slapped one hand over my eyes and reached for Baba with the other, but all I could grab was his walking staff.

Then just as suddenly as it had started, it was over and everything was deathly quiet. For several seconds I couldn't move. Somehow the bullets had missed me. When I finally opened my eyes, I saw the terrorists in the distance, running toward Dark Mountain. Without looking, I reached again for Baba, but he wasn't there. I slowly turned and saw him huddled on the ground beside me. "Baba, Baba, what's wrong?!" I cried.

He groaned in pain as blood oozed from his side, turning the dusty street from brown to dark crimson. Youssef lay nearby in a lifeless heap. Ibrahim had escaped by diving through an open window into his shop.

Mama and my sisters rushed from the house to Baba's side as neighbors and friends came to help. Ibrahim ran to the town's only telephone and called for an ambulance. Karya Maghola was only a small village and the nearest hospital was in Asyut, so it would be two long hours before it could get to us. Time seemed to stand still, and I wanted to shout, *Why doesn't somebody do something?* But there was very little anyone could do but wait.

The minutes slowly ticked by and Baba remained remarkably calm. He tried to reassure Mama that he would be all

right. "I am okay, don't be afraid. God will take ca...
he said. Then he prayed, "Dear God, I place my w...
children into your hands."

While all of this was happening, Mama knelt by his s...
occasionally bathing his face with a wet towel. I watche...
from nearby, and I could tell things were bad. Once I heard
Baba whisper to Mama, "If . . . if something should happen
to me . . ." A cold shroud of fear began to wrap itself around
me, and I thought, *What does he mean "if something should
happen"? Nothing* ever *happens to Baba.*

When the ancient ambulance finally arrived, they gently
lifted Baba onto its bed and put him inside. Mama squeezed
in next to him and I tried to follow, but they wouldn't let me.
The door slammed shut, and as the ambulance wobbled its
way back down the rutted street I began to sob, "No! No! I
have to go with Baba!" Ibrahim gently took my hand and led
my siblings and me to his house next door.

Friday night was filled with bad dreams and terrible memories. Images of Baba's bleeding body were seared into my
mind. Saturday passed in a fog. The heat and dust didn't
even bother me and I wanted nothing to eat. I kept asking
about Baba, but no one would tell me anything. When the
sun rose on Sunday, it was no better. There would be no
worship service that day in Karya Maghola. How could we
worship without our beloved pastor?

Early that evening Mama returned home, accompanied
by a few close friends. Several neighbors saw her arrive, and

to meet her. When she walked upstairs to our
here was no one there. "Where are my children?"
ked. One of her friends explained where we were, and
said, "Please bring them to me."

When I heard Mama was home, I was so happy. *Now
I will see Baba!* I thought. But when I ran into our house,
he wasn't there. As I frantically looked around the room, I
saw many men's faces, but not Baba's. Everyone was crying,
including Mama, and she was dressed in black from head to
foot. I had never seen her like that before. I ran over to her,
but when I looked into her eyes, it seemed she was in some
faraway place. My mind was filled with so many questions
that I thought it would explode. I still didn't understand
what had happened; no one had told me anything. Finally I
couldn't keep things inside any longer.

"Mama, Mama, where is Baba? I want to see him, is he
all right?" Mama didn't answer.

"You can't see him now," Baba's friend Jakub replied. "He
is not here."

"I know he's not here, but where is he? I want to see him!"

"He's in heaven with Jesus, Nathan. But don't worry, you
will see him again someday." Then he tried to hug me and
calm my fears.

I roughly pushed him away. "I don't want to see him *someday*. I want to see him *now*!" Then I burst into tears, whirled,
and ran from the house.

When a person dies in a village in Upper Egypt, they are

buried at once, usually in the town where they were when Mama came home on Sunday, Baba's funeral and burial had already taken place. No one had both to explain this to me. But that evening, I slowly begar understand what had happened on Friday. When the ambu lance took Baba away, it was for forever. He was gone, and he would not be coming back. He wouldn't be there to pray for our Friday breakfast or to lead children's church. There would be no more walks with Baba through the streets of Karya Maghola. Never again would I see Baba here on earth, and I knew that never again would Friday be my favorite day.

Later that evening, I slipped back into our house and watched from the shadows as a steady stream of friends and neighbors came to comfort Mama. I had been in the homes of most of these people, but I had never seen them act this way before. It seemed like the dreary procession would never end. The black clothes, the sad faces, the tearful prayers . . . the longer it continued, the worse I felt. Mama tried to be kind to our friends, but how can you be kind when your heart has been ripped out?

Finally, I couldn't watch any longer. No one seemed to notice when I quietly retreated to my room. I stood at my window and watched the sun slowly slide below the horizon. As the sky faded from orange to purple and then to gray, evening shadows—like slithering snakes—began invading the empty streets of Karya Maghola. In the distance the devilish face of Dark Mountain mysteriously reappeared, and it seemed

ghing at me. Now I understood why people said it
1. It was the place where the wicked gunmen lived.
one in my room, I tried to sort through the jumbled
zle of the last three days. For a while my thoughts just
emed to get more confused. I slowly began to discover answers to one set of questions only to have others elbow their
way to the front of my mind. *How could you let this happen,
God?* I wondered. *Didn't Baba tell me you are a good God,
and wasn't Baba serving you? It just isn't fair!*

These are questions that no six-year-old boy should be
forced to ask, and as they swirled in my head, I felt something new bubble up in my heart. Everything that had been
bottled up inside for three days overwhelmed me, and hot,
angry tears burst from my eyes.

With vivid images of Baba's vicious killers still cycling
through my memory, I clenched my fists, raised them over
my head, and shook them toward Dark Mountain. Then
as the dark curtain of a desert night slowly descended on
Karya Maghola, I breathed a passionate warning to the two
terrorists—bitter words that should never come from the
lips of one so young.

"Someday," I whispered fiercely. "Someday I will have a
gun. And when I do, I will *find* you, and I will *kill* you, because *you killed my Baba*."

2

WEDDING BELLS

1916–1944
UPPER EGYPT, NEAR ASYUT

My story actually begins many years earlier, in another village called El Sahel, the home of my grandparents. Everyone in the region was poor, and they worked hard each day just to scratch out a living. My grandfather was named Bassaly, but people referred to him as the Man of Prayer, for even though he had no formal education he was very wise and looked to God for direction in every area of life.

Most of the men in El Sahel were farmers, and they hoped for many sons to help with the work. Daughters were all right, but they were expected to stay at home and help with the

ᷤehold chores. In fact, the arrival of a baby girl was not ᷤsidered all that important to village families. The birth ᷤ a son had much greater significance—especially for the father: it validated his manhood.

Grandfather Bassaly was a carpet weaver, and he kept a small loom in his home. Although he was a good craftsman, his business provided barely enough income to support his small family. Within the first years of their marriage God blessed my grandparents with two children, a daughter in 1917, named Erada, followed a year later by a son named Latif. Sadly, when the young boy was only four years old, Grandmother became quite ill. Medical care was not available in El Sahel, so over the next several weeks her health continued to decline until she finally died. Grandfather Bassaly found himself with two small children and no wife to care for them.

While struggling to adjust to his new situation, Bassaly heard about an American missionary's home for boys in the city of Asyut. He investigated further and found the home also enrolled the boys in a nearby school. This immediately got Bassaly's attention, since in those days village children had little opportunity to go to school. The more he considered the matter, the more he wondered, *Could this possibly be God's answer for Latif?* He submitted an application for his son, and it was quickly approved.

A few weeks later young Latif found himself in a strange new world. Asyut was a fair-sized city situated along the

Nile River, quite different from the sleepy village where he was born. There were lots of shops, lots of people, and lots of hustle and bustle. But the biggest change was living in a house with ten other boys. It was nice to have so many "instant friends," and he soon found himself thinking, *This place is really great.*

From the first day of class, Latif was one of the best students. After finishing secondary school he found that education was becoming more common in the villages around Asyut. Although he had not attended university, he discovered he was qualified to become a teacher. When Latif was offered a teaching position in the village of Shotb, he quickly accepted. He soon learned that he was the only person in the region who could read and write other than Father Paul, the local Coptic priest. This meant that in addition to his teaching he would also serve as the leader of everything that happened in the entire district.

When Latif began looking for a place to live, Father Paul offered him a room above the church. It would be a bit cramped, but how much room did one man need? A warm and lasting friendship began between the two men, and their relationship provided opportunities for my father to develop both his teaching and preaching skills.

Latif soon found that teaching children was a very satisfying life for him. He enjoyed the close bond he had with his students, and as time went by he also built strong relationships with their parents. Before he knew it, the calendar had moved from the 1930s to the '40s, and he was approaching his twenty-fifth birthday. And although occasional news reports of distant wars were heard in Shotb, people in the villages of Upper Egypt wasted little time worrying about such things.

———

In 1943, while Latif was enjoying his busy and happy life in Shotb, Hyat, a young girl from a nearby village, was nearing marrying age. Although Latif had never even heard her name, she would soon quietly enter his life and things would never be the same.

Hyat was not like most village girls. She came from a religious family, and this gave her a special position in the eyes of the community. She had even attended primary school, which was unusual for girls in those days. Her grandfather was a Coptic priest, and she often accompanied him to meetings with church leaders from the region. That's where she met Father Paul and his wife, Tassony.

According to Egyptian family customs, parents played an active part in finding mates for their sons and daughters. Father Paul's daughter was about the right age for marriage, and the pastor had mentioned earlier to Latif that she might be a good wife for him. However, when the suggestion was gracefully declined, Tassony came up with a new idea. There was this young girl in a nearby village who would be just perfect for their teacher-friend.

With Latif's permission, Tassony contacted Hyat's parents, who indicated they were open to such a proposal. A meeting was arranged, and soon Latif was on his way to meet with the girl's family. The closer they came to Hyat's village the more nervous Latif became, and a whole series of questions cycled through his mind, such as, *Will her family like me?* and *I've never seen this girl. Is she really as beautiful as they say?*

Accompanied by Tassony and his sister Erada, Latif arrived at Hyat's home to find her entire family waiting. As Tassony made all of the proper introductions, Latif's eyes scanned the room, trying to pick out his prospective bride. When he saw Hyat, he thought, *Yes! She will be my wife!* However, members of her family were not so sure, and they launched an intensive interrogation.

"How old are you?" "How do you earn a living?" "Where will you live?" They fired all sorts of questions at Latif, but what they really wanted to know was: Is this man good enough for Hyat? Is he someone we can invite into our family?

When the relatives finally ran out of questions, the meeting ended with a sumptuous meal. The women of the family had been cooking all day, and the menu included both chicken and beef, an extraordinary treat. Nothing was too good to celebrate the possible engagement of their dear Hyat. When it was time to leave, the family gave no indication of whether the marriage proposal would be accepted. So all Latif could do was return home and wait for further word.

A few days later a message came from Hyat's family inviting Latif to come again, and to bring only his father. This was a good sign, and he immediately ran to share the news with Bassaly. The Man of Prayer was also pleased, and a few days later Bassaly and Latif arrived at Hyat's home. This time they carried simple gifts: a few live chickens in a cage and a ring for the potential bride-to-be. Her parents greeted them at the door, but Hyat was nowhere to be seen. These parental negotiations would determine if the young couple would be allowed to marry.

The nervous prospective groom sat listening as several topics were discussed, practical things such as: Where would the wedding be held? *In the village of Latif's family, of course.* How would Latif support his new wife? *As a teacher of children.* Where would the newlyweds live? *In Shotb, where Latif currently lives.*

After these matters were resolved, other topics were raised—things like who would perform the ceremony, who would be on the guest list, and who would prepare the wedding feast. Some were not questions that required answers; they were more like village customs that needed to be observed. When it seemed there was nothing else to discuss, Hyat's father voiced one final requirement that was not open to compromise. Since his daughter was only fourteen years old, the engagement period would be one full year. Bassaly readily agreed; but to Latif, one year sounded like an eternity.

Once Hyat's father had agreed to the marriage, he summoned his daughter from the next room. When she appeared in the doorway, Latif instinctively rose to meet her and his heart began to race. A blush of pink slowly spread across his face as he thought, *She is no fourteen-year-old girl. She is the most beautiful woman I have ever seen.* He continued to stare as she walked toward him, but her shy eyes did not look him in the face. When she reached his side, they both turned to face their parents.

The moment for the formal act of engagement had arrived. Hyat's parents took their place on one side of the couple and the Man of Prayer moved to the other side. Bassaly nodded ever so slightly to Latif, who reached into his pocket for the ring. It was a simple gold band.

In Egyptian culture, this ring holds great meaning. The unending circle of gold symbolizes eternal love between a husband and wife. On that day it was an engagement ring; one year later it would become their wedding band. Latif handed the ring to his father, who placed it on the fourth finger of Hyat's right hand. Then he offered up a prayer, asking God to bless this couple and grant them a long life of peace with many children.

While this was happening inside, excitement was building outside also. The attention of the whole village was focused on Hyat's house. Everyone knew there were visitors from another place, and they knew why they had come. Hyat's girlfriends were gathered in small groups around her house, and some of the less timid ones even crept up to peek in the front window. They wanted to see this Latif with their own eyes. Was he really a suitable match for their friend? And what did a Man of Prayer look like, anyway? Maybe like the picture of Jesus in the church. They were so excited they couldn't stop talking. Chitter-chatter, chitter-chatter—they sounded like a flock of chickens.

It was now time for the two families to celebrate their commitment with a private dinner. When they had finished eating, Hyat prepared and served black tea, and all the while Latif looked for any small excuse to be near her. But conversation between the two was still not permitted. When everyone had finished their tea, the parents voiced satisfaction with the wedding arrangements, made small talk about Latif's next visit, and said their goodbyes. Then father and son set out for home.

At last Hyat's girlfriends had their chance to see Latif. A few called out words of congratulation as he and his father walked along the street. One or two disappointed young men whispered less than complimentary remarks about this intruder from Shotb. The groom-to-be again felt a warm flush creep up his face. He only relaxed when they rounded a bend in the road.

Over the next year Latif visited Hyat as often as possible. The more time they spent together the more convinced he was that she was God's choice for him, and their relationship slowly changed from two shy strangers to a trusting and loving couple. But one thing did not change: they were never allowed to meet without others present, since casual dating was not a part of Egyptian life. Latif and Hyat would always be accompanied by a proper chaperone until the day of their wedding.

As the world turned the page of its calendar from 1943 to 1944, few people knew or cared about what was taking place in Upper Egypt. World War II raged on across Europe and the Pacific, and the failed effort of Benito Mussolini to annex North Africa was becoming a distant memory. But none of this really mattered to Latif. He just wanted to complete his courtship and get on with the wedding.

After numerous visits and countless hours with Hyat, Latif assumed that all the preliminary wedding customs had been fulfilled. But then another message arrived from her father, calling for one final discussion between the parents. *We settled everything months ago*, thought Latif. *What else is there to discuss?*

Once again Latif and his patient father set out for Hyat's village. On this visit the families would finalize a detailed blueprint for the entire marriage celebration. Since this stage of planning was mainly women's work, Hyat's mother quickly took charge of the proceedings. She made a series of suggestions and Bassaly simply agreed, since it appeared the decisions had already been made long before he and his son arrived. It all seemed rather boring to Latif. He just wanted to know two things: where the wedding would be held, and when he was supposed to show up. Once he heard them agree to a date in May, Latif's thoughts wandered to other things. He began to imagine what life as a married man would be like. No more fixing his own meals or going home to an empty room. He was tired of all these delays. It was time to move on to his life with Hyat.

The days leading up to the wedding became increasingly busy for Latif and Hyat. The groom looked for ways to rearrange his tiny bachelor's room to accommodate a couple. Also, Erada insisted that he upgrade his wardrobe, and that meant a shopping trip to Asyut.

Hyat also had a to-do list. She would make her own wedding gown and assemble cooking utensils and household items for their new home. She would take these with her when the family traveled to El Sahel for the wedding, since she would not be returning to her parents' home after the ceremony.

The weekend of the great occasion arrived at last, and everything seemed ready. Now it was time for family and friends to join in the festivities. Two grand and glorious parties were organized for the couple on Saturday: one in Hyat's village for the bride and her girlfriends, the other a bachelor affair in Shotb honoring Latif. The music and dancing continued well into the evening, and by the time it was over everyone was exhausted.

Latif awoke Sunday morning feeling rested and relaxed. He had no reason to be concerned about the day's events. He was only the groom, and all he had to do was dress up and show up. He got out of bed and tried to eat a bit of breakfast, but he wasn't hungry. So he gathered his new clothes and other essentials and headed for his father's house.

Such relaxation was not the case for Hyat. She was awake long before sunrise. Outside her room the family was bustling about, making last-minute preparations for their journey. As she nervously began putting on her wedding gown, her mother generously showered her with last-minute advice. The bride hardly heard a word her mother said, but she injected an occasional "Yes, Mama" just to keep the conversation moving. When every bow and ribbon was in place, her mother nodded her approval, and the shy young bride joined the rest of the wedding party in the sitting room. It was time for the long and elaborate processional to El Sahel.

When Hyat's family arrived at the outskirts of El Sahel, an official reception party was waiting. A sleepy-looking camel with wrinkled skin knelt nearby, decked out in colorful fabrics with a tent-like affair on its back. Hyat and her two bridesmaids were soon inside that tent, hidden behind its long, flowing curtains. The camel awkwardly rose—first the back legs, then the front—and began moving down the street in his ambling, swinging gait. Other than Hyat's entourage, the village streets were abandoned.

When they arrived at the church, the nervous groom was waiting outside. The camel knelt and Hyat's father drew back the curtains. Standing before Latif was a stunningly beautiful angel, and before he knew it she was beside him. The nervous couple turned and walked inside. No wonder the streets were empty. The entire village had been jammed in this hot, stuffy church for two hours. When they saw the bride and groom, they rose to their feet and began clapping. The women cried out with ear-piercing Arabic ululations—high-pitched, trilling sounds of celebration. When the wedding party reached the front of the room, they all settled back into their places, men on one side of the room and women on the other. When everyone was completely quiet, the pastor began the service.

"Brothers and sisters, we are gathered here today in God's sight to unite Latif and Hyat in holy matrimony." The words were so familiar the groom could have recited them by memory. As the pastor's rich voice filled the room, Latif's thoughts again began to drift. The service seemed to go on for hours. Suddenly the groom was jarred back to reality when he heard: "Do you, Latif, take this woman to be your wife, to have and to hold . . .?" When the pastor paused, Latif turned to Hyat and firmly replied, "I do!"

The same questions were repeated to the bride, and again there was a pause. This time several seconds ticked by and no one moved. Finally Hyat turned to Latif, looked into his eyes, and softly whispered, "I do." An audible stir drifted across the room.

The pastor then asked, "Latif, what do you bring to seal these vows?"

"A ring," he replied. He took it from Hyat's right hand and passed it to the minister, who held it high and explained its symbolic meaning. Then he returned it to Latif, who placed it on Hyat's left hand. She repeated the solemn ritual with a second ring for Latif. The pastor then proclaimed, "I now pronounce that Latif and Hyat are husband and wife. What God has this day united, let no one ever separate."

A shiver of excitement ran from Latif's heels to the top of his head. *Husband and wife!* he thought, and the words continued to echo in his mind. Before anyone could move, the pastor raised his hands and said, "Now I ask Brother Bassaly to come and pray our benediction." Latif's father stepped forward and placed his hands on their shoulders.

When Bassaly finished praying, he slowly turned the newlyweds toward the congregation and proclaimed: "It is my great privilege to present to you, for the first time, this new family of Latif and Hyat. May the God of heaven keep them safe for years to come, and may he give them many sons and daughters. Amen!" Once again the room erupted with applause and ululation.

When things calmed a bit, Bassaly invited the entire congregation to join them for the wedding feast, and that's when all order and decorum seemed to evaporate. Some started pushing their way toward the newlyweds to offer congratulations. Others had more practical things in mind and made a mad dash for the best seats at the dinner tables. Before things got completely out of hand, the pastor stepped forward and ushered Latif and Hyat to the head table, followed by their parents and the rest of the wedding party.

Hours later, when the last of the guests finally departed, the bride and groom were completely exhausted. Hand in hand, they made their way to Bassaly's house, where they would spend the next two nights. All day Monday a stream of well-wishers came with wedding gifts, usually small sums of money. Then early Tuesday morning it was time to set out for home. Latif took one look at the mound of belongings Hyat had brought and thought, *How can one so young accumulate so much?* Then he bundled some of the most necessary items into two packs, a large one for himself and one of a more manageable size for Hyat. The rest would have to wait until later.

A hot desert sun in a cloudless sky relentlessly pursued Latif and Hyat along the winding road to Shotb. The farther they walked the hotter it became, and the heavier their packs seemed to be. Salty perspiration soaked their clothes and traced tiny trails down their dusty faces. When they approached the outskirts of the village, a new crowd of friends was waiting to greet them. It was the last thing they wanted.

"Just look at me," muttered Hyat, "I'm a mess." And while they knew the people meant well, they were both thinking the same thing: *When will we ever get to be alone?*

3

A SON! A SON!

1944–1955
SHOTB TO ASYUT

Latif and Hyat enjoyed a few days of relative calm after arriving in Shotb. It felt good to be away from the hustle and bustle of the past month. But soon the pace picked up again and their lives started getting busy. Latif resumed his teaching at the school and church, while Hyat tried to invent ways to fit all of their belongings into a one-room flat. When it looked like she might have the problem solved, she remembered the things they had left with Bassaly.

"This will never do," Hyat declared. "One room may be fine for a single man, but it's much too cozy for a couple.

And where would we find space for a baby?" So she began a search for more suitable housing.

In a few days Hyat discovered what she was looking for: a two-room flat. It wasn't the perfect solution, but two nice rooms would be a big improvement. When she told Latif what she had found, he readily agreed to move. If this would make Hyat happy, then he would be happy. They transferred their belongings to the new flat, and a few days later they made a fast trip to collect the things they had left in El Sahel.

Once their housing crisis had been resolved, Latif could concentrate on his teaching. It was no wonder the students loved his classes and dreamed of life beyond their tiny village. His creative use of drama and other nontraditional teaching methods challenged them to excel. One of Latif's most enthusiastic students was Mousa, who went on to earn a degree in engineering. He often told people, "Effendi Latif was the best teacher I ever had." Many of Mousa's classmates agreed, and they also went on to prestigious professions such as architecture and education. But Latif was most proud of those few bright students who felt called by God into lives of Christian service.

Hyat also began putting her education to good use. She started helping Latif at both children's church and the school. It wasn't long before mothers from the village began coming to her for counsel in many areas of family life: how to raise children, relationships with husbands, problems with neighbors, and other practical matters. It was an area of ministry that would become the trademark of her life.

Before they knew it, Hyat and Latif had been married for one whole year. On the evening of their anniversary he came home to find his favorite meal waiting, with an extra portion of tender chicken. After dinner Hyat brought two cups of hot tea and sat down beside him. He settled back and let his mind drift over the events of the past year. *This is the life*, he thought. *How could anything be better?* But when he glanced at Hyat, he could see she had something on her mind, though she didn't say a word.

Finally Latif's curiosity got the best of him, and he asked, "Hyat, you seem to be bothered tonight. Is something wrong?"

"Oh no, I'm fine," she replied, then shyly looked down at her hands.

"Come now, Hyat, you can't keep secrets from me. What is it?"

She looked at him and said, "All right, I'll tell you. When we married, do you remember something we both wanted?"

"We wanted a whole list of things. Which one do you mean?"

"Well, there was one that was extra special. Don't you remember?"

After a few seconds a light turned on in Latif's mind. He reached for his wife's hand and whispered, "Hyat, are you telling me . . ." And he couldn't say it.

"Yes, Latif, you are going to be a father."

He couldn't believe his ears.

Latif had a hard time waiting for the glorious day to arrive. He was teaching one morning when a message arrived saying to come home—and quickly. He dismissed the class and dashed from the school. When he got home he was greeted by a flurry of activity. The midwife hustled him into the next room and left him there. *I feel so useless*, he thought. *I want to do something!* But all he could do was pace and pray.

A few minutes later Latif heard a tiny cry. He turned and saw the midwife beckoning. His heart leaped for joy as he thought, *He's here!* But when he heard her words, his heart sank.

"Congratulations, Father, you have a baby girl."

They named their daughter Hoda, but it would take some time before he could accept this as God's answer to their prayers. The next year the Lord blessed them with a second daughter, Phoebe, and soon their neighbors began to say, "Poor Latif, only girls. When will he ever have a son?"

The months flew by and the pace of Latif's life continued to increase. Because he loved the people so much, he started taking on more and more responsibility for them. He became increasingly frustrated as he tried to balance full-time teaching with part-time ministry. Then one day another unexpected offer was thrown into the mix: the Coptic bishop invited him to become a priest. Latif's head was swimming, and for the first time since moving to Shotb he wondered if God had something else for him to do other than teach. He tried to pray, but his prayers didn't seem to go anywhere. Finally he decided to have a talk with his father. Surely he would know how to solve this dilemma.

After Latif explained his problem, Bassaly said, "You really are asking two questions, my son. First, I would advise you not to take the path leading to the Coptic Church. Teaching their children is one thing; becoming a priest is a different issue.

"As to the second matter, no one can know the Lord's will for another person. You must discover your own God-directed path, Latif. So I would advise that you and Hyat seek an answer directly from God himself." With those words, the Man of Prayer sent his son back home.

That evening Latif sat down with Hyat and poured out his heart to her. After many late-night discussions and hours of prayer, God made it clear that they should be in full-time ministry. This meant leaving a comfortable life in education and stepping into an uncertain future. It also meant leaving Shotb and spending the next few years at the Bible school in Asyut. But once the decision was made, the peace of God filled their hearts and they started planning for the days ahead.

Latif now had to share his decision with the church, his students, and the rest of the village. Everyone was shocked. How could Latif leave Shotb? He was more than their teacher; he was their friend. And who would their wives go to with their problems? Some tried to convince them to change their minds, but when they saw that talking wasn't working, they quietly made an action plan instead.

The day finally arrived for the move to Asyut. With heavy hearts, Latif and Hyat began to carry furniture from the house and load it into a donkey cart. It was then that their friends put "Plan B" into motion. As fast as someone would carry things *out* of the house, someone else would carry them *back in*. They weren't trying to be difficult. They simply couldn't bear to see these dear friends leave.

The comical parade went on until Latif finally called a halt and asked everyone to gather around. After a tender time of prayer, they finished loading their belongings into the cart and said one final farewell. Then, with salty tears blurring their vision, the young couple set out with little Hoda and Phoebe for their brand-new life in Asyut.

Shortly after Latif applied for admittance to the Bible school, two important things happened. First, he was offered a part-time position as pastor of a small church near the school. He could attend classes Monday through Wednesday, then pastor the rest of the week. The church provided both a modest salary and a small flat for his family. The second blessing was related to his academic requirements. The Canadian missionaries who directed the school decided that because of his background, he would be enrolled in the second year of the program, not the first. That meant he could complete his studies in three years rather than four.

Latif could hardly wait to start the fall term. In addition to the regular program, he studied both Hebrew and Greek. His marks were excellent in every subject, but more important were the extra elements of his life. He became known as a caring and compassionate person, with a soft and loving way. He also distinguished himself as an outstanding preacher and Bible teacher.

––––––––––

One day, as Latif was nearing his last year of classes, he came home to find his wife waiting at the door. It didn't occur to him that she wanted to talk. His mind was still working on the Hebrew lesson his professor had presented that day. After listening to her husband try to explain a sticky Hebrew phrase, Hyat interrupted him.

"Latif, please! Forget about your Hebrew and come sit down. We need to talk."

"Of course, my dear. What is it you want to say?"

"Well do you remember how we have prayed for a son for all these years, and God has given us only daughters?"

"How could I forget? But you know I love Hoda and Phoebe, and I'm trying to be patient."

"I know, Latif, but I think maybe God has heard our prayers."

"Hyat, are you saying we will have another child?"

"Yes. I've suspected it for some time, and for some reason I'm more hopeful this time."

"But why didn't you tell me sooner?"

"I didn't want to raise false hopes. And besides, you always seem to be so busy."

"I know, but I'm never too busy for this kind of news. So let's thank the Lord for answering our prayers, and then let's be more specific. Let's promise that if we should have a son, we will give him back to God, just as Samuel's mother did back in Bible times."

After they prayed, Hyat made her husband agree not to tell anyone of her pregnancy for a while. However, within days he had shared the secret with a couple of close friends, and it wasn't long before everyone in the neighborhood knew. But by then the birth time had nearly arrived, so it really didn't matter.

When Hyat knew delivery was near, a midwife was called. Asyut was a big city, but she never even considered going to a clinic. She wanted this baby to be born at home, just as her two daughters had been.

As her pains became severe, Hyat worried that she would have another girl. She wanted so much to have a son, for Latif's sake. He had prayed so hard for so long, and Hyat felt she had disappointed him too many times in the past.

When the little one arrived, the midwife exclaimed, "Oh Mother, you have a baby boy!" Latif heard her in the next room and rushed in to see for himself. After making sure that both mother and son were fine, he raced outside and began spreading the news.

From her bed, Hyat could hear Latif shouting at the top of his voice: "It's a son! It's a son! At last I have a son!" Then he rushed to a nearby shop and bought some tiny bottles of

Coca-Cola to share with everyone. It was an extravagant thing to do, but who cares at a time like that?

When Latif finally came back, he sent word to their families and invited them to come. As for Hyat, she just cuddled the tiny boy and silently thanked the Lord for answering their prayers.

As news of the new arrival spread, the whole neighborhood became a beehive of activity. Ladies paraded to the house carrying roasted chicken, sweet dark honey, fresh-baked bread, and other delicacies. There would be a great celebration that day at the pastor's house.

The next morning the new parents were required to register their son's name at the Bureau of Records. Family members began a lively debate, proposing first one name and then another, until Latif rose from his chair and ended the conversation. The room became silent and everyone waited to hear what he would say, since his decision would be final.

"Thank you for your suggestions, but Hyat and I agreed months ago that if God should send us a son, we would call him Nathan, which means Gift of God."

Latif left at once for the government office as the ladies began setting out large platters of food. But no one would eat a bite until the proud papa returned home.

After that day lots of things changed for my parents, including their names. Everyone stopped calling my father and mother Pastor Latif and Hyat. Instead they were known as Abu Nathan and Om Nathan, the father and mother of

Nathan. But as I grew up none of this really mattered to me. While I loved Mama dearly, my devotion to Baba was even stronger. I always looked up to him, and in my eyes he could never do anything wrong. And that's the way it would remain, for as long as he lived.

4

LITTLE BOY, BIG DREAMS

1956–1962
ASYUT TO KARYA MAGHOLA

Within a few days of my birth, life returned to its normal busy pace in our home. Baba was juggling his pastoral responsibilities and his final year of biblical studies. As the demands on his time grew, he sometimes felt trapped in a hopeless tug-of-war.

Meanwhile, Mama also resumed her daily routines, with only a few adjustments for a third child. But one thing caught her completely off guard: just as she was settling into her new schedule, women began arriving uninvited at our door. They had been coming to Mama for counsel before I arrived, and they were ready to resume their meetings. Why let a little thing like childbirth interrupt their plans?

As Baba dug more deeply into the Bible, he became fascinated with scriptural references to the country of Egypt. Two of these are found in the book of Genesis, when Abram and Joseph each traveled there. Later, in Matthew, Mary and Joseph took Baby Jesus to Egypt to escape King Herod's slaughter of the young boys in Bethlehem. Each year throngs of people still visit a large cave outside Asyut where it is believed the holy family once lived.

Baba also discovered that Christianity was first brought to North Africa by Mark, author of the Gospel bearing his name. He was sent there by the apostle Paul after their journey to Colossi. When Mark arrived in Alexandria in AD 49, he immediately established a church, and both the Coptic and Orthodox traditions trace their Egyptian roots to this event. After ministering in other places, Mark returned to Alexandria in AD 68, where he was martyred for his faith. Sadly, the practice of violence against believers still continues nearly twenty centuries later.

During his student days Baba often preached at a village church in the small town of Kom Abas, not far from the Bible school. One day just after his graduation, leaders from the village came to Asyut looking for Baba. They found him at home, and when they arrived at our door, Baba invited them in. After a bit of casual conversation the men explained the reason for their visit. The church in Kom Abas was without a pastor, my father had been highly recommended, and they had come to offer him the position.

Baba could not have been happier. It would be his first full-time pastorate, and he could put into practice everything he had been studying. Best of all, he would no longer need to spread himself between two jobs; he could focus all of his attention and energy on ministry. After several more discussions over the next few days and many hours of prayer, Baba accepted their invitation.

Once again a spirit of excitement invaded our home. At the same time, there was a twinge of sadness as Baba and Mama packed up our meager household belongings. Just as when they moved from Shotb, they would be leaving friends behind. It was especially hard for Baba, who would lose relationships at both the church and Bible school. But for my mother, leaving the city and returning to village life was like moving back home.

The next two years in Kom Abas were happy times for our growing family. It was there that my third sister, Sawsan, was born. Still, in spite of the demands of four energetic youngsters, Mama continued to devote countless hours to the mothers and children of the village, just as she had in Shotb and Asyut. And Baba's sincere and loving concern for people, coupled with his dynamic preaching, drew an ever-increasing number of families to the church. God's presence was truly in that place.

After two years of fruitful ministry, Baba again heard God calling him to a new ministry in a place called Mishta. When he announced this news to the church on the following Sunday, people were disappointed, but it wasn't quite as difficult for my parents as when they left Shotb. At least this time there was no parading in and out with the furniture. Meanwhile, Mama began to wonder if moving would always be a regular part of her life.

My first clear boyhood memories begin with our time in Mishta. Like most pastors' homes in Upper Egypt, our house was on the second floor above the church. The place was a little snug, with only three small rooms for a family of six, but the worst part for me was sharing a room with three sisters.

Since we had nowhere else to keep our goat, it lived right in the house with us. Mama was not at all pleased with that arrangement, but I thought it was great. For the first time in my life I had my very own pet. Finally one morning Mama loudly proclaimed, "Nathan, if you like that smelly goat so much, then you will take care of it."

Baba was often gone all afternoon visiting families throughout the village and beyond. He counseled them in both spiritual and business matters and was highly respected for his wisdom. When he came home, he would tell Mama all about his day. His activities may have seemed ordinary to someone else, but not to me. I began to dream of tagging along, but Baba insisted I was too young and no amount of pestering could change his mind.

On most days when Baba left the house, I would drag a chair to the front window, climb up, and watch for him to return. As soon as he appeared up the street, I would run outside to meet him, calling out, "Baba, Baba, you're home!" He would break into a wide smile, swing me in circles, then set me down and give me a couple of candies. I felt like the luckiest boy in the whole world.

In many ways Mishta was a lot like the last place we had lived. It was a community of farmers, with long days of hard work. It's not easy to make plants grow in such a dry climate. Baba sometimes offered practical suggestions to his neighbors, and they were surprised that a pastor actually knew about farming. But that was Baba. He used any avenue to build relationships and open doors for ministry.

Mishta also introduced several new elements to our lives. I remember seeing my older sisters dressed in their school uniforms, running out the front door. They simply could not wait to see their teacher. I wanted to go too, but they said, "No, little Nathan, you are not old enough." So I begged Baba to fix it. When he had heard enough, he went to talk to the headmaster, who agreed to let me attend "unofficially," as long as I did not take part in class.

The most important change, though, was in Baba's ministry. The church in Mishta had services every evening, and Baba preached them all. I still remember families coming in and taking their seats, men on one side of the room and women on the other. When the other children ran outside to play, I always remained in the service, watching and listening to everything my father did and said. He was my superhero, and I dreamed of the day when I would be a pastor just like him.

Daily life settled into a regular routine for me. I spent my weekday mornings at school, and after a while Baba began to take me along on his afternoon visits. Then during the evening services, I sat in a chair behind my father with my Bible open on my lap. I still couldn't read, but that made no difference to me. The adults didn't seem to mind this unusual behavior. Some of them even said, "My, that Nathan is different from the rest of the children, very grown up for his age."

Shortly after our move to Mishta, Mama became pregnant again. Since I was still the only son in the family, I decided it was time for some divine assistance. "Please, dear God," I prayed, "this time make it a baby boy." Baba was praying for the same thing, but for a more practical reason. He was thinking, *How could I ever support four daughters with only one son to help me?*

On the day the baby arrived I experienced the first big answer to prayer of my life. At last I had a brother! When they told us, I started jumping for joy, but Baba was even happier. He began to exclaim, "Glory to God, you have heard our prayers!" And this time there was no family debate to select a name. "We will call the boy Magdy," he said, "because that name means 'glory.'"

Life was just about perfect for me at this point. I had friends, I was going to school, and I was "helping" Baba with his ministry. Then at the end of two years, a pair of special events happened very close together. First, my youngest brother, Onsey, arrived on the scene. Then just after my sixth birthday, Baba announced that God was again leading us to leave Mishta and move to a new church. Suddenly my perfect life was turned upside down.

It was pretty hard for me to understand what Father's "God-is-leading-us" words meant, so I decided to ask him, since he knew everything. I can still remember him chuckling softly as he picked me up and held me close.

"Nathan, you have such big questions for such a little boy. Let me try to explain. You see, son, it's like this. When I was a small boy like you, my father told me a story about a man named Abram. Do you remember him? The Bible says God talked to Abram one time and said, 'I'm going to send you to a place where you have never been before.' And God didn't even tell him the name of the place. But when he heard God speak, do you know what Abram did? He did exactly what God told him to, then trusted the Lord to take care of him, no matter what happened.

"Then my father told me something I have never forgotten. He said, 'Latif, if you will always go wherever God tells you to go and do what he tells you to do, God will take care of you, just like he took care of Abram. He will always bless your life, and I promise nothing will happen to you that God does not allow.'

"Now, Nathan, God has never spoken aloud to me like he did to Abram, but I still believe those words of my father. I know if I go where God tells me to go he will always take care of me, no matter what comes along. And I can promise the same will be true in your life. If you always follow God, then nothing—and I mean nothing—will ever happen that is not for the best. And that explains why we are moving to Karya Maghola. Now run along, Nathan, you've asked enough questions for today."

Baba's answers always made sense, but this one seemed extra special. *Always follow God, and nothing will happen that's not for the best.* That was a pretty big thought for me, and I still didn't fully understand it, but I decided to stop worrying about it and start behaving like a grown-up. *After all*, I thought, *I'm six years old, and I need to act like it.* So I tucked Baba's words away until later and ran outside to find my friends.

Over the next several days, Baba told us what life would be like after we moved. Our new home would be in Karya Maghola, a village I'd never heard of, and Baba made it sound like the most wonderful place ever. We had always lived close to the beautiful Nile River, where most of the people were farmers. Now our home would be in the shadow of distant mountains. It all sounded very exotic to me—until we got there.

The wagon carrying my family bumped its way into town, and my heart sank as I surveyed the scene. No matter which way I looked it was dry and desolate, with a dull brown blanket of dust coating everything. Once again our house was above the church, and when we pulled up in front, it seemed okay; but when we got inside, I was in for a big disappointment. It did have four nice-sized rooms instead of three, but it also had a third-level rooftop patio for our animals. I thought, *You mean my goat will no longer live inside with me?* I was crushed.

Baba had not shared some of the less pleasant things about Karya Maghola with us children. The village was really not the best place to raise a family, and the church had been without a pastor for quite some time. The entire region had a bad reputation and no one wanted to live there. While most of the people were hard-working and trustworthy, there were some—especially those living out near the mountains—who were believed to be involved in dark and dangerous activities. Baba had discussed all of this with Mama, and they both agreed that since God had led us here, then he would take care of us. All the same, I suspect that deep in her heart Mama had some serious misgivings.

As we settled into our new home, there was a feeling from the first day that life would be different in this place. I never doubted for a minute that people would fall in love with Baba, and indeed that began with the first church service. His warm and caring spirit reached out to greet his new church family, and they quickly returned his love. As for the rest of us, we soon accepted even the heat and dust as part of our daily routine. Mama got the house in order, and in a few days Baba took my two older sisters to enroll them in school. When he inquired about me, he found I was eligible to become an official student too. I couldn't wait for the first day of classes.

When the fall term began, I resumed my daily routine: mornings in the classroom, afternoons with Baba, and evening church services. Once again I dreamed of following in Baba's footsteps, and before long I found myself thinking, *You know, this place is going to be just fine. We may live here for a long time.*

For the next few months, Baba's ministry flourished, and I followed him everywhere. Soon people began saying, "Here comes the pastor. Where is his shadow? He can't be far behind." Mama was busy raising six energetic children and interacting with the mothers of the community, who often gathered at our house on Friday mornings during the children's church services.

Before we knew it, we had lived in Karya Maghola for six months. I was now able to locate the Scripture passages Baba used in his messages, and I was also familiar with most of the Bible stories he referred to. But one Sunday morning he got me completely confused when he started telling the people a story about me! I didn't even try to find it in my Bible, because I knew it wasn't there.

As I sat behind him in my usual spot that morning, I could hardly believe my ears. He told the people Nathan was very wise, someone who heard God's voice. I thought, *What is he saying? I've never heard God's voice.* Then he said I had a friend named King David. When I heard that, it really upset me because I didn't know anyone named David. He went on to say that this king had done some bad things, and God told Nathan all about it. Then God sent him to tell King David, "You are the man!"

The longer my father preached, the more frustrated I became. After the service, I couldn't wait for the last person to leave so I could talk to Baba. When we were alone, I ran up to him and blurted out, "Baba, why did you lie today? That story about me was not true. I don't even know a man named David. You have never lied before, Baba. How could you stand up there and say things like that?"

My father burst out with the biggest laugh, then took me upstairs and called for the family to gather around. Mama was busy fixing our meal, but Baba said it would have to wait. There was something he needed to explain to the children. Then he opened his big Bible and introduced us to King David of Israel and his friend Nathan, the prophet.

When Baba finished, he turned to me and said, "So you see, Nathan, I wasn't lying at all. The whole story is right there in God's Word. In fact, now you know where we got your name in the first place. So what do you think of that?" I didn't know what to say. After a few seconds, Baba ruffled my hair and said, "Enough sermonizing for now. Mama, it's time you served our Sunday dinner."

That message became one of my most treasured memories from childhood for two reasons. First, I had never dreamed there was actually a "Nathan" in the Bible, and that made me feel very special. But the second reason was much more important, and I really didn't realize it until after the following Friday. That's when I discovered it was the last sermon Baba would ever preach.

5

SHATTERED INNOCENCE

The distant crowing of a neighbor's rooster told me a new day was dawning again in Karya Maghola. The morning sun was just beginning to peek from behind Dark Mountain as I rolled over on my lumpy sleeping mat and tried to go back to sleep. But then it hit me: Baba's booming voice would not be calling me to breakfast that morning, or any other morning for as long as I lived. Soft rays of sunlight started invading my room, but the dark shadows that had engulfed me for the past three days refused to surrender.

It had been another long and lonely night. My whole world was now one scrambled mess, with countless questions no one seemed willing to answer. As I lay in bed that morning, my mind began to replay the past three days, and the pieces of my puzzle just wouldn't fit together.

I remembered the ambulance coming to take Baba away, and his soft moans as they lifted him onto that strange-looking bed. I recalled trying to squeeze in beside Mama before the door closed, and Ibraham gently pulling me away. That's when I caught one final glimpse of Baba. Then loneliness engulfed me as the ancient ambulance wobbled its way down the empty street.

As the sky slowly brightened, my thoughts skipped over Saturday and landed on Sunday. *Was it really only yesterday?* I had waited all day for Mama to come home, thinking when she did Baba would be with her. But he wasn't. I kept asking where he was, but every time the answer was the same: he wasn't coming back, he had gone to heaven.

At first I didn't understand what they meant, but by the end of the evening I had figured it out. "Gone to heaven" really meant "gone forever." Baba was never coming back—not tonight, not any night. *How can this be?* I wondered. *The Bible says when someone goes to heaven, you are supposed to be happy. So why isn't everyone happy?*

Then there was Mama. She had always walked around with a smile on her face. But not that night. She just wandered from room to room as if she were lost. And that ugly black dress—I hated it. Every time she saw me she started crying again. She kept patting me on the head and saying, "It's okay, Nathan, it's okay. Believe me, everything is going to be okay." I wanted to shout, "No, Mama, it's not okay! How can you keep saying that?"

The sun soon turned my room into an oven, so I forced myself to get up. I pulled on my *galabayya*, then wadded up my sleeping pallet and dumped it in a corner. I didn't feel like folding it properly, and what difference did it make? No one had paid much attention to me or anything I did since Friday.

When I went to get some breakfast, the house was full of strangers. There were relatives we hadn't seen in years, friends and neighbors from Mishta and Shotb, people from the Bible school in Asyut—and lots of people I'd never seen before. They kept coming in a never-ending stream, and most of them were wearing those ugly black clothes, just like Mama. And whenever someone new arrived, they would all start crying again.

I only heard fragments of their conversations that day, and the words I did catch were really strange. They said things like: "Don't worry, Mother, God will take care of you," "Our God will see you through these dark days," and "All of this will work out somehow, Sister." But the words that upset me the most were, "We are praying that God will make things right." I wanted to scream back at them: "Make things *right*?! How can things *ever* be right when those evil men have killed my Baba?" But a six-year-old boy doesn't do that. He just jams those angry thoughts deep down in a back corner of his heart.

Strange people . . . strange clothes . . . strange conversations—that pretty much describes the entire day. It was almost more than I could handle. My whole world was shattered and I didn't know how to fix it. Never again would Baba swing me in circles or come and pray with me at bedtime. There would be no more walks together, no more listening to him preach.

From that day on, I slowly began to understand that we had to get used to life without Baba. But just because I understood it didn't mean I had to like it. Then one morning my threatening words from Black Friday came back to me: "Someday I will find you and I will kill you."

That was the day I started seeing life in a much different way. A fountain of bitterness began to bubble in my heart, and sometimes my hatred was so strong it would pour out in hot, salty tears. Other times, when no one was around, I would shout vile threats at the terrorists. If anyone had heard me they would not have been surprised, because revenge is an everyday part of the culture in my part of the world. Since the terrorists had killed Baba, I knew it was my sacred duty as the eldest son to kill them back. So I began thinking of ways to get even. I knew this kind of behavior didn't match up with what Baba had taught me, but at that point I really didn't care.

I thought maybe things would get better after I decided to seek revenge, but they didn't. Gruesome images of guns and blood cycled through my mind, and there was no way to escape them. Nights were the worst. Visions of leering, angry people invaded my room, and I often cried out in terror, knowing they wanted to kill me. When Mama heard my heartrending sobs, she would rush to my room, hold me in her arms, and rock me, hoping to chase away my fears. After a few minutes I would drift off to sleep, only to have it all start again in a few hours.

Days were not much better. Everywhere I went my eyes scanned people's faces, hoping to see Baba, but of course that never happened. Slowly I became well acquainted with a word I had heard many times: *death*. In the past it had been something that happened to other people. Now it had invaded my life, and it wouldn't leave me alone.

Days turned into weeks, and angry, hate-filled thoughts continued to occupy my mind. At the same time, there were other thoughts competing for my attention. They started as a soft whisper, and at first I tried to ignore them. But they continued to grow louder, demanding that I listen. It slowly dawned on me that these were familiar Bible verses I'd learned in children's church, solemn words like "Vengeance is mine, says the Lord, I will repay," and "Love those who hate you." But it wasn't long before I shoved aside these lessons. I didn't want to love my enemies. All I wanted to do was kill them.

I really had two Nathans living inside me, and they were battling for my soul. There were times when I paid attention to Good Nathan and tried to obey what I had been taught. But to be honest, there were more times when the voice of Bad Nathan drowned out the good.

Then one day, as this war raged inside me, I heard a third voice. This time it was Baba's voice, and it reminded me of the talk we'd had before we moved to Karya Maghola. It was as if he were holding me on his lap just like he had that day and saying, "Nathan, do you recall what God told Abram? He said, 'If you follow me, nothing will ever happen that is not for the best.' So no matter what happens in your life, you must keep believing that promise." Keep believing? How could I? All I wanted to say was, "No, Baba, it's just not true. Don't you know what happened here on Black Friday?"

Those words continued to trouble me for days. *Always follow God. Nothing will happen that is not for the best.* Then I finally decided it was time to drive Baba's words from my head and let Bad Nathan take control of my life.

My childish decision now put me in an uncomfortable spot. I had this boiling passion for revenge bubbling in my heart. My mind was filled with visions of getting my own AK-47, going out to Dark Mountain, finding the terrorists, and blowing them away. My imagination kept inventing plan after plan, each one more bloody and violent than the last. I didn't know when or how I was going to pull it off, but there was one thing I did know for certain: it was going to happen.

Alongside my secret life, I had to maintain my super-clean "Baba's-little-boy" image on the outside. I couldn't let people find out about the Bad Nathan. If they did, what would they think of me? I also knew that if Mama found out about my plans for revenge, she would be devastated.

As if this turmoil wasn't enough, another conflict began to press in on me. After Baba's death, people often said, "Well, Nathan, now you are the man of the family. You are the one who will replace your father." At first, I didn't give it a lot of thought. I was too busy dreaming up my plans for revenge to worry about what other people said. But after hearing this time after time, the pressure to provide for the family began to get to me. I'm sure they didn't mean to force me to instantly become an adult, but that's what it sounded like to me.

Then one day my mind flashed back to my father's final sermon, the one about Nathan and King David. I remembered Nathan's harsh, accusing words to his friend: "O King, you are the man!" That phrase really frightened me. Were the prophet's words also meant for me? I didn't want to be a man; I wanted to keep on being a boy. Nathan's words kept ringing in my head for days, and I started thinking, *I've lost another piece of my life. I've lost my childhood.*

6

BYE-BYE, KARYA MAGHOLA

A month had gone by since Baba's death, and I was still wandering around in my own little world of troubles. Meanwhile, Mama was wrestling with much bigger problems. She found herself with six children under the age of twelve to care for, and no income. One day she was a happy wife and mother and the next she was forced to confront a paralyzing question: *How will I feed my family?*

The immediate solution to this problem came from neighbors and friends. Day after day their generous outpourings of love kept us abundantly supplied with delicious meals.

Magdy and I would often try to sneak into the kitchen for a taste of some new dish. Our sisters wanted to do the same, but they were too timid.

In spite of such compassionate care, life in our home was a monotonous parade of empty days. Each morning my personal dark cloud hovered overhead, waiting to surround me. Mama kept most details of our desperate situation hidden from us. But there was one serious matter she could not hide, something that left her nearly in a state of panic.

When Baba became pastor in Karya Maghola, the church provided a house. Now that he was gone, that would no longer be true. It all came down to one simple fact: no pastor, no house. As soon as Baba's replacement was found we would have to move, and Mama had no idea how to solve this dilemma.

The husband's relatives were expected to find solutions to such situations, so what started out as Mama's problem soon became a full-blown family debate. While it was mainly the men—brothers, cousins, and nephews—who dealt with these issues, I can assure you the women freely injected their words of wisdom into these discussions. Animated negotiations were conducted right in our home, and there was no effort to keep us children from listening in. It was disheartening to hear our family haggled over like some commodity traded at the neighborhood street market.

Most of these discussions revolved around some very practical and legitimate concerns, things like: "I really do love

Latif's family; but we have barely enough to feed ourselves," and "I already have nine in my family. How can I add seven more?" Finally the men threw up their hands in frustration and admitted they had failed. Everyone gathered around Mama to offer sincere apologies for not coming up with a solution, and after a sad farewell they left her to wonder, *What am I going to do now?*

A few days later, an elder from the church came with distressing news: the leaders had found a new pastor, and he would be coming soon. For two months the church had graciously allowed us to stay in their house, but now we would have to move out within a matter of days. Mama still had no place for us to go, and on top of that, school was about to start and she needed to know where to enroll her children. Mama felt there was no one in Karya Maghola she could talk to, so she did what she had always done in the past: she talked to the Lord.

A few days later a retired pastor and longtime family friend arrived at our door. Mama invited him in, and he could see that she had been crying. My sisters went to fix tea, and I snuggled up next to Mama in the sitting room, expecting another one of those dreary "I'm-so-sorry" conversations.

After expressing his condolences, the pastor said he wanted to read a passage of Scripture. He reached for his Bible and turned to 2 Kings 4, which tells the story of a widow with children and her conversation with the prophet Elijah. The woman in the story explained to Elijah that all she had to feed her family was one jar of oil, and when it was gone she didn't know what she was going to do. I thought, *That sounds like us.*

When the pastor finished reading, he closed the Bible and looked at Mama. His next words were kind and filled with tender compassion. "Sister, you and your family have been heavy on my heart, and today I have come with words of encouragement for you. I want to say that our God has not changed since the beginning of time, not in Old Testament days, and not in our day. He provided for the widow and her family in Elijah's time, and I can promise he will care for you." Then he sat quietly for a moment. When he spoke again, he seemed to be choosing his words carefully.

"I have been thinking and praying much about your situation, and I believe the Lord has revealed a solution for your problem." He paused once more—a bit longer this time—then began again. "I believe what God wants to tell you is this: 'My child, the best thing for you, and also for your family, is to move . . . to Cairo.'"

Mama was stunned. "Cairo! *I* can't move to Cairo. It is a big city, and I have never even visited such a place. Pastor, you know I am a village woman. How will I ever survive in a big city?" The tears flowed again, and she buried her face in her hands.

The pastor wisely waited for Mama's emotions to ease; then, in a gentle and loving way, he explained his thinking. In a big city like Cairo there would be many more opportunities for Mama to start a new life, opportunities that she would not have in the villages she knew so well. There were fine schools for her children, and also a good church that would welcome her family into fellowship. He had even talked with some Christians who had moved from Karya Maghola to Cairo, and they had offered to find a place for us to live.

Mama and the pastor talked for a long time. As our friend painted a colorful and inviting portrait of what life would be like in the city, I thought, *You know, Cairo doesn't sound so bad to me*. After listening to the pastor's words, Mama also seemed more relaxed than she had been in weeks.

When there was nothing more to be said, the pastor suggested Mama take some time to pray about "the Cairo plan." Then if she agreed it was the right decision, he would make all of the necessary arrangements. After promising to stay in close touch, he gathered us around for a parting prayer. When Mama came back from walking him outside, I could see a shy, uncertain smile in her eyes. I wanted to smile too, because for the first time since Black Friday, I felt a tiny bit of hope deep down inside.

Within a day or two Mama concluded that the Cairo plan was the right solution for us. Once her decision was made, she wasted no time putting the plan in motion. First, she sent word to the pastor asking him to prepare the way. Next, she gathered her children to tell us all about the move. Then, with the help of a few close friends, she started packing. Although she had moved several times in the past, this would be a much different pack-up than before. Mama said we could only take the bare essentials, since she didn't know what our city flat would be like. I thought, *What are you worried about, Mama? If we are moving to a big city, surely we will have a big house.*

On the day of our move, a friend volunteered to drive us to Asyut, where we would board the train. Our furniture would stay behind with neighbors, to be sent later. Sadly, I also had to say goodbye to my goat. We gathered outside the house with our friends for one final farewell, then climbed in the car. Suddenly a lump welled up in my throat as I thought, *I'll probably never see these people or this place again.* As we drove out of town, I turned to watch our house slowly disappear behind us. Then I buried my head in Mama's lap and fought to hold back the tears.

When we arrived at the train station, family members and more friends were waiting to see us off. Mama purchased our tickets, and then we all stood around pretending everything was normal. I'm afraid we weren't a very happy-looking lot. Soon we heard the wail of the train whistle as it approached the station. As it rolled to a stop, everyone started crying and clung to each other with final, loving hugs. Then the whistle tooted again, and we had to pull ourselves away and board the coach. Our seats were in third class, so when we got inside the car it was crammed full. But after Mama's negotiating and some pushing and shoving, we finally got seats together. It could have been a lot worse. Many people had no seats, so they had to stand in the aisle all the way to their destination.

As the train rolled out of the station, it seemed like my life was ending. We were leaving the only world I had ever known. Happy childhood scenes drifted through my memory: riding the bus to Asyut for my first haircut, visiting the candy shop for sweets, playing games with friends. But then those memories were washed away as reality swept over me. I thought, *We're nothing but a bunch of wandering nomads. We don't even have a home.*

The wheels of the train clattered a hypnotic cadence as we rattled our way toward Cairo. *Clickety-clack, clickety-clack,* they chanted. I had expected my first train ride to be exciting, but it wasn't. The landscape continually faded from river-bank green along the Nile to desert brown, then back again. Through it all, one phrase kept cycling through my mind, matching the beat of the wheels: *leaving-my-home, never-return . . . leaving-my-home, never-return.* It wasn't long before I began drifting in and out of sleep. There was no curiosity about Cairo; it was a name that meant nothing to me. I only knew we would be stuck on this hot, over-stuffed train for the next nine hours with no air-conditioning. The windows were all propped open and the stifling heat made life miserable for everyone.

The train was powered by an old-fashioned steam engine, and it spewed out a cloud of foul-smelling black smoke and powdery gray soot. This mixed with the ever-present desert dust to create a dingy layer of grime that covered everything and everybody. From time to time the whistle wailed its warning as we approached another village. I don't know why. There didn't seem to be anyone or anything moving outside, as far as the eye could see.

Our train chugged on, mile after mind-numbing mile. After two or three hours, we older children began to push and pick, bicker and fuss, making life miserable for those around us. Mama tried to keep us corralled, but it was impossible. As things were about to get completely out of hand, assistance suddenly appeared from a most unexpected source.

Sitting across the aisle from us was a young man wearing a long *galabayya*. After watching Mama's ongoing struggle with her children, he finally asked her if he could give us some small candies. The look of relief on her face said it all. With a friendly smile the man held up a bag of sweets and said, "Children, look what I have!"

Suddenly, six pairs of eyes were glued to that bag of candy. The man passed it around and encouraged us to take not just one, but several. Magdy and I grabbed as many as we could hold and stuffed the extras in our pockets. Then we popped a couple in our mouths and savored the sugary taste.

Now that some semblance of order had been restored, the man returned to his seat and began to chat with Mama. His home was in Cairo, and he was returning from his engagement party in Asyut. When he said he was a Christian, Mama was not surprised. To her, he was like an angel sent from heaven, and

I'm sure the other passengers in our coach would have agreed. This gracious gentleman shared his food with our family, played games with us, and kept us distracted for the rest of the trip.

When the train finally chugged into the Cairo station, we were more than ready to get out of our rolling prison. Clutching our parcels tightly, we elbowed our way to the door and stepped outside, where we were immediately swallowed up by a pushing, shoving throng like none we had ever seen. Across the way, several people I didn't recognize began to wave. Obviously, they were expecting us.

With the help of our train angel, we slowly managed to muscle our way through the crowd to where the welcome committee was waiting. They greeted Mama with friendly handshakes and assured her that everything had been arranged for us. So we said goodbye to our new friend, thanked him again for the candies, and watched him disappear into the crowd, never expecting to see him again. Then we gathered up our packages and set out for the flat that would be our new home.

As we walked out of the station we were immediately swallowed up in a surging sea of humanity. As far as the eye could see the streets were jammed with buses and cars, donkeys and goats, and endless people all in a hurry to get somewhere. At times the traffic even spilled onto the sidewalk, sending people scrambling to safety. I thought, *So this is Cairo. It sure isn't like Karya Maghola*.

We walked for quite some time and soon found ourselves in what seemed like a really dangerous part of the city. All around us were dingy little shops, scruffy-looking people, and narrow alleyways filled with all sorts of junk and rubbish. But the main thing that captured my attention was all of the huge, high buildings towering around us. Our friends led us into one that was at least six stories tall. I thought, *Wow! Things really are big in Cairo, aren't they?*

Inside the building were long, tunnel-like hallways leading in several directions. My eyes immediately spotted a strange-looking button on the wall of the entryway. Like all boys, my curiosity got the best of me and I pushed it. Instantly, a whole bunch of bright lights flashed on. "Look, Magdy," I said, "they have a generator here, just like our church in Karya Maghola." I had never been in a place where "real electricity" came through wires in the wall.

We followed our friends up to the second level, then down a hallway. When they stopped in front of an open door, I couldn't believe my eyes. We found ourselves staring into the tiniest two-room apartment that we could imagine. It would be my home for the next twenty-five-plus years.

As darkness began to settle over the city, our new friends told us goodnight and promised to come back the next day. When they were gone, we unpacked our few belongings and got ready for bed. Once we had wiggled our way onto our tightly-packed sleeping pallets, Mama turned out the light. As I drifted off to sleep, I thought, *Well, I guess everything in Cairo is not going to be big after all.*

7

STARTING OVER

My first morning in Cairo I was not awakened by a crowing rooster. Instead, it was all the sounds that invaded our flat: horns and bells, banging pots and clanging pans, slamming doors, running feet, and loud voices. When sleep was no longer possible, we fumbled our way through a simple breakfast and ventured out to explore the neighborhood.

Over the next few days my eyes were opened to a whole host of amazing discoveries: getting water from a tap, cooking in an oven instead of over a wood fire—an endless list of surprises. But there was one thing that was way too much for me to comprehend.

One day, while sitting in our flat, I heard strange music and voices coming from someplace nearby. My curiosity was aroused, and an investigation was definitely in order. I went out to the hallway, and in the flat across from ours I saw a big black box with a shiny glass face sitting on a table. Inside it were tiny people moving about, and that's where the music and voices were coming from. A boy about my age was sitting in front of the box, so I asked him, "What is that?" He gave me a strange look and replied, "It's a television, silly!" I had no idea what he was talking about.

For the first few days life in our tiny flat about drove us crazy: two rooms, seven people, and lots of noise—always lots of noise. None of us got much sleep, and we all longed for our calm and quiet home back in Karya Maghola.

Outside was no different. Wherever we went there were crushing crowds of people, all rushing in different directions. Traffic in the streets was one huge tangle of donkeys and horses and buses and trucks and cars, with a generous number of dogs and cats thrown in. Some of the cars had funny blinking lights on top, which my "TV friend" told me were called taxis. I wasn't about to ask what those were.

It was a mystery to me how Mama kept everything together, but she did. On our third day in Cairo, she announced it was time to find a school for us, and she put my oldest sister in charge while she was away. As she headed out of the flat, I caught up with her at the door and asked, "Mama, can I go with you . . . *please*?"

Following directions from a neighbor lady, we started our search. When we had gone only a short distance—maybe two or three blocks—I saw a familiar face in the crowd. It seemed too good to be true. "Mama, Mama," I exclaimed, "there is the man from the train!" I began pushing my way over to him, and as Mama trailed along behind I couldn't help thinking, *God, you have done it again.*

When our friendly angel saw Mama and me, his face broke into a big smile. "Would you look who's here? Why are you in this part of town, Sister?"

"We live in a flat just a few blocks down that way."

"Where are you going now?"

"To enroll my older children in school. A neighbor gave me directions, but I'm afraid I didn't listen closely. I can't seem to find it."

"It isn't far. Come, let me show you. And on your way back home, you must stop here. This is my grocery shop, and I will make sure you have the things you need."

When Mama finished our school business, we retraced our steps to the grocery. Our new friend had already started a large pile of items he thought we could use. Mama began to protest that she could not buy so much, but the man told her not to worry; he would take care of it this time. Our arms were full when we left his store that day.

By the end of the first week, our city life was coming together rather nicely. We now had a school and a friendly grocer, and we were getting adjusted to our tiny apartment and all of the noise. Then on Sunday morning some of the folks who had welcomed us at the train station came to escort us to morning worship. When we arrived the people greeted us warmly, just as the retired pastor had promised back in Karya Maghola. Things were definitely looking up.

As days became weeks, I slowly started thinking of Cairo as my home. With so many new things to distract me, I gradually became accustomed to our new normal. My little black cloud no longer greeted me each morning when I awoke, and the dark circles slowly faded from around Mama's eyes. But the one thing that did not change for Mama was that horrible black dress. According to the custom of her generation, she continued to wear it for many years.

The worship center quickly became an important part of our lives. It was not really a church like the ones we had known in the south, since it didn't have a full-time pastor and was a much smaller congregation. (Something else in Cairo that was not big.) But one thing was just the same as before: Friday children's church. This is where I met two special ladies, wonderfully gifted teachers who had invested their lives in ministry to children just like me.

Every Friday morning these two ladies showed up in our neighborhood, where they went door-to-door inviting boys and girls to a time of fun and games. As they walked down our street they soon had a troupe of happy children trailing along behind. The farther they went, the bigger the troupe became, and when I saw them I immediately wanted to join the parade. I hadn't laughed and played that way for months. There was one thing we didn't realize at the time though. These ladies had a specific goal in mind: they were gradually herding their flock toward the church.

Once we arrived at the worship center, we all gathered around our teachers, anticipating a new and exciting adventure, and week after week they never disappointed us. They always came up with such creative activities. The most exciting time for me was when they brought out a "magic light box" that could shine pictures on the wall. As one teacher told a dramatic Bible story, the other illustrated the scene and projected it for us to see.

One Friday, our teachers began sharing the story of a famous man named King David. I thought my heart would explode. I remembered the Sunday of Baba's last sermon, and it was almost as if he were standing there telling the story again. When my teachers went on to tell about David's friend Nathan, I wanted to jump up and say, "That's me, that's me!" But I was afraid everyone would laugh, so I didn't.

Over the next weeks and months, I attended every single worship service and children's church meeting. But there were still two Nathans living at our house. There was the one on the outside who was nice and kind and obedient, who studied hard and memorized all of his Bible verses. But inside, in a dark corner of my heart, there was that other Nathan. He was still broken and angry—angry with the world, with his life, even with God—and I kept him securely locked in a place where no one could ever find him. No one, that is, but God.

Obviously I was still full of the hatred I had carried with me since Black Friday. I still had a burning passion to get a gun and go after the terrorists. For a long time I thought I could just keep both Nathans around and change from one to the other when it suited me, but that was simply not possible. Sooner or later, one of them would end up controlling me.

By this time I had become very close to my two dear teachers. They patiently taught me about the way Jesus loves everyone, even the ones who do bad things to us. Gradually I found myself wanting to be more like Jesus. At the same time, Bad Nathan kept whispering in my ear, *You are not Jesus; you don't have to love everyone—especially not those evil terrorists.*

Once again, there was a battle raging in my heart, and I'm sure my teachers were wise enough to sense this. But they continued to plant the seeds of Jesus's love in the soil of my heart. As they did, the Parable of the Sower recorded in Matthew 13 began playing out in my life, but in a slightly different way. This time the parable played out in reverse, as the *good* seeds of God's love grew up and choked out the *bad* seeds of hatred planted there by the terrorists. But for a long time my sinful desire for revenge refused to surrender.

One evening, around the time of my twelfth birthday, this battle became too much for me to handle. So I told Mama I was going to the adult prayer service at church, which was my usual habit. The meeting had already started as I quietly slipped inside and found a secluded spot where I could kneel and pray.

As I knelt there that night, the burden of hatred and passion for revenge weighed heavily on me. I remembered what Baba used to tell people: "You must pray and invite Jesus to come and live in your heart." Finally, in the quiet of that tiny sanctuary, I quietly whispered, "Jesus, I invite you into my heart tonight. Please wash me in your blood and heal my inner wounds. Change me, dear Jesus, and make me just like you."

Several minutes passed, and nothing happened. Then a new Voice whispered softly in my ear. It said, *Nathan, from this day on you are my son. But if you truly want to be like me, you must get rid of the hatred hiding in your heart and forgive those evil men who killed your father. Only when you have done this can you begin to be like me.*

For the next several minutes I waited quietly before the Lord. Then, for the first time in five years, I turned off the voice of Bad Nathan and breathed another simple prayer: "Jesus, I forgive those terrorists, I really do. Please come right now and wash away my hatred."

When I opened my eyes, everything around me was new: the walls of the church were new, the faces of the people were new. As I ran out the door and back to our flat, everything along the street looked new. When I burst through the door, Mama took one look at me and could easily tell something had happened. I ran into her arms and the words poured out.

"Oh, Mama, I'm new! Ever since Black Friday there have been two Nathans, but now there is only one. I'm a new Nathan. I've been born again!"

The date is burned forever in my memory: October 9, 1967. It's the day I moved from jihad to Jesus.

8

THE NEW NATHAN

When I awoke the next morning, my life was totally changed. While images of Baba's bleeding body and visions of masked gunmen continued to visit me, my whole attitude toward the terrorists was different. The hatred I had been hiding in my heart for five years was gone, and it had been replaced with a true spirit of forgiveness. I remembered the words of Jesus as he was hanging on the cross: "Father, forgive them; they don't know what they are doing." I asked Jesus to give me that same kind of heart.

I became a serious student of the Scriptures, and soon it began to bother me that many of our church services were led by people with little Bible training. I often thought, *Baba could have taught this lesson much better.* Sometimes I even wanted to jump up and correct the leader.

One evening, our study leader read a passage from 2 Timothy 4. When he was finished, he invited anyone to tell the group what the Scripture meant. Without thinking, I stood up and began explaining the apostle's words. I boldly stated that Paul was talking about Timothy in these verses.

Feeling quite proud of myself, I returned to my seat. When no one said anything, I thought, *They must be dazzled by my wisdom.* Actually, they were confused. In a few seconds another brother stood and said, "Nathan's explanation of these verses was totally wrong. Here is what they really mean." Then he spent several minutes correcting my errors and rebuking me for speaking out of turn. The longer he spoke, the louder he became, and by the time he finished I wanted the floor to open up and swallow me alive.

After the meeting some other believers came to encourage me. One of them said, "Don't worry about tonight, Nathan. You are a good boy and we know you are serious about following Jesus. At least you have the courage to speak up, even around older Christians. Someday, when you are ready, God will reveal his plan for you." That evening an impulsive teenage boy learned a valuable lesson.

The load of family responsibility began to wear on Mama, but she never complained. Raising six little ones made it impractical for her to find a job; besides, working outside the home was culturally unacceptable. Still, Mama was not one to sit around doing nothing, so when she was asked to lead the women's Bible study, she immediately accepted.

God continued to faithfully provide for our family in a variety of practical ways. While the church gave Mama a small widow's pension, it wasn't even enough to pay our rent. So some Christian friends who knew our situation organized a regular monthly fund for us. They became God's hands to take care of his loved ones.

Our generous grocer continued to be one of our Good Samaritans too. We did all of our shopping with him, and he gave us a special discount. Every time Mama came home from the store she would find a few extra items in her bags she hadn't asked for. Best of all, at least for Magdy and me, were the juicy watermelons we often found at the bottom of the bag.

Another generous gentleman was a medical doctor who helped us in many ways. Two times each year when he really got my attention were Easter and Christmas. That's when he would come to our house and drive my brothers and me to a place that made custom leather shoes. His big, shiny car would roll right up to our front door and we would proudly climb in. As we drove away, people would stare and wonder what made us so important.

The wonderful smell of leather would greet us as we walked in the door of the shoe shop. The cobbler always carefully measured our feet then showed us the glossy leather he planned to use. And he always had some tasty treats for us before we piled back in the car for the ride home.

One week later, we would go back to the shop to pick up our shoes. We were always so excited when he handed us our own shoeboxes. We would clutch them so tightly you would have thought they were full of money. No one could pry them from our hands. For several nights when we went off to bed, we would take our new shoes with us—right inside the box.

When we had been living in Cairo for about six years, I was about to complete my final primary school term. I was one of the top students, no doubt because I had tagged along to the village school with my sisters when I was very young. This gave me a head start on the rest of the students in my class, and since school was a lot of fun for me, I studied hard and earned high marks in every subject.

Near the end of the term I was picked for a contest to name the best boy student in our school. Most of our classes included girls, but they were not allowed to participate. When the contest ended, I was not surprised to be named the winner. Without meaning to sound arrogant, that's simply how I thought it would turn out. Then my teacher informed me I would compete against boys from ten other schools. The winner would receive the outstanding primary student award for the entire district. So much for my self-confidence. I would have to work much harder to have any chance to come out on top.

The day of the competition arrived, and the arena was jammed. Everyone was dressed in their school uniforms, and I wore my shiny church shoes—the ones the doctor had bought for me at Easter. The judges led the contestants onstage and we took our places. When the final round of questions was over, we were told to remain in our seats. It seemed like forever before the judges reached a decision, and my stomach was in knots.

Finally the head judge stood and said, "Today we have a small problem. Two boys are tied for first place." He paused and the arena went silent. Then he read the names. When he said my name, I couldn't believe it. Then I wondered, *Now what?*

The judge called for attention before continuing. "We have decided on a simple way to break the tie. Each contestant will answer one more question, and whoever gives the best answer will be our champion." The other boy went first, and after he gave his answer the judge turned to me and said, "Nathan, solve this riddle: What walks first on four legs, then on two legs, then on three legs?"

For a few seconds, my mind went blank. Then two clear images came to mind—one in which my baby brother was crawling on the floor, and the second of my father walking with his cane. So I stood, nodded to the judges, and said, "Sirs, here is the answer. It is a man. As a baby, he crawls on hands and knees; when he grows up, he walks on two legs; when he is old, he must use a walking staff." Then I sat down.

The judges leaned together and whispered for a minute. Then the chief judge rose and said, "Our winner is Nathan. Congratulations." Students and teachers from my school began to chant, "Our school is best! Our school is best! Nathan has won top prize!" I was very pleased to win the award, but I was even more pleased when I was told this award also qualified me to continue my education at prep school.

There were several prep schools in Cairo, and I was assigned to one reserved for the best students. That was good for educational reasons, but not from a practical sense. The school was quite a distance from our flat, and it required a city bus ride each day. The daily commute was hard to get used to at first, but after a while it almost became a game. I would watch for bus 82 to come around the corner, then join the wrestling match to get aboard. None of this taking-turns business; it was every man—and boy—for himself. If you were not aggressive, you waited for the next bus. And I quickly discovered the headmaster didn't listen to "bus excuses" if we were tardy.

One Thursday in December of my final year, I was running a bit late. As I ran up the street I saw old number 82 rolling to a stop and I knew it would take an extra-special effort to make it on. When the doors opened the pushing and shoving started, and just as I was about to squeeze through the door, someone slammed into me. The next thing I knew, I was on the pavement with my left arm in the path of the bus.

When the bus suddenly lurched forward, someone screamed and the driver stopped—right on my arm. When he backed up agonizing pain shot through my body and blood gushed onto the street. I stared at the crimson pool and my mind flashed back to that day in Karya Maghola. Paralyzing panic seized me and I thought, *I'm going to die in the street, just like Baba!*

Some people turned away, unable to watch, while others pushed forward, wanting to help. I heard the wail of an ambulance in the distance, but I had no idea if it was coming for me. Then a lady in the crowd recognized me. "That's Nathan!" she screamed, and ran to find Mama.

The next thing I heard was someone shouting, "Stand aside, here is the mother!" As the crowd pulled back, Mama saw me in a pool of blood and collapsed at my side. "No, God, nooo!" she sobbed. "First Baba, and now Nathan. It is too much, dear God!"

Just as someone said, "It's no use; he'll never make it," two strong arms reached down and scooped me up. The man was a total stranger, but he immediately took charge. "Stop that taxi!" he shouted. "Come, Mother, we must find a doctor—now!" Then I passed out.

I faintly remember being lifted onto a white cart at a government hospital. This was the lowest possible medical treatment available in my country; but Mama didn't care and neither did I. All I wanted was for the pain to go away. As soon as we got inside, they rushed me to surgery and took Mama to a waiting area as a merciful cloud of unconsciousness enveloped me again.

The doctor worked frantically on my arm to stop the bleeding. After trying several different procedures, he concluded there was only one thing that might save me: he had to amputate. But to do this, he needed permission from a parent or guardian. Leaving me on the operating table, he rushed to the waiting area.

"Where are the boy's parents?" he barked.

The receptionist pointed. "His mother is there; he has no father." Still dressed in his blood-spattered gown, he hurried to Mama and spoke to her in a harsh voice.

"Woman, I have done all I can to save your son's life, but it does not look good. The only hope left is to amputate his arm. Will you permit it?"

"Doctor, I don't know what to say. Let me think for a minute," she replied.

"There is no time to think, Mother, you must decide *now*. If I don't amputate at once, your son will die."

Mama was so confused. She didn't want to lose me, but she didn't want me to lose my arm either. So she breathed a silent prayer: *Help me, Jesus; show me the way*. At that moment, a supernatural peace enveloped her. Turning to the doctor, she said, "Sir, I cannot permit it. My answer is no."

Without another word, the doctor whirled and marched back to the surgical room. "Just patch him up and put him to bed," he snapped. "He won't make it through the night."

Two days later I awoke in a dingy room with two other patients, needles and tubes running everywhere. When Mama saw my eyes open, she brought a wet cloth to bathe my face. After a few minutes I drifted off to sleep again.

Nothing changed for the next two months. I was too weak to get out of bed, and as I tossed and turned, one question kept playing through my mind: *What will my life be like now?* I was only fourteen and my dreams were destroyed. I prayed constantly for God to heal my broken body.

When nothing happened, I became impatient. *Why wouldn't God answer me? Didn't he care?* I even blamed him for my situation. My prayers sounded something like this: "I am a good person, God; I have given you my heart. I've been studying your Word, and look where it has gotten me. This is all your fault." Sometimes I complained to Mama and my family, but usually I kept these thoughts to myself.

One afternoon a surgical cart rattled into my room and stopped at the empty bed beside mine. Nurses gently lifted a boy about my age from the cart, laid him in bed, and tucked him in. When the nurses left, he went right to sleep.

After a while, I heard the voice of a different boy outside my room. Each day he would walk down the hall calling, "Tea and coffee, tea and coffee." He seemed nice enough, but I could tell he was poor and uneducated. That afternoon when I heard his sing-song chant, I grumbled aloud again.

"God, there is that simple boy again, walking up and down the hall selling tea and coffee. And look at me; I can't even get out of bed. Please, Lord, at least let me walk around saying 'tea and coffee' like him."

Then I heard a loving, almost-audible voice whisper back, *Nathan, you will not be a tea-and-coffee lad. I have other plans for you.* The voice seemed so real I thought the boy next to me may have heard it. But when I looked over at him, he was still sleeping.

Later I heard someone singing, and this time the sound was coming from the next bed. When I looked over at my roommate, he was wide awake, with a big smile on his face. He tried to turn toward me, but it was too painful.

"Hello, who are you?" he said.

"My name is Nathan. What's yours?"

"I'm Mohammed. Who were you talking to a minute ago?"

"I was talking to God. I told him I'm not happy with what has happened to me."

"Why are you here?"

So I told him my whole sad story: the bus, my arm, the fact that I couldn't even stand on my own legs. It all just gushed out, and then I added a few bitter words about the hospital.

"I've been here two months, and nothing they do makes me better. What brought you here? You don't seem too sick to me."

He continued to smile as he said, "Can't stand on your own legs? Take a look at this." Then he raised his sheet, and I saw he had only one leg. "I was running too, trying to catch a streetcar. I also fell and slid under the wheel, and when I didn't move fast enough, it ran right over my leg. My doctor didn't need to amputate. His work was already done."

I felt like someone had punched me in the stomach. I had been complaining to God for weeks because I couldn't stand, and here was this boy just like me, with only one leg to stand on. It was time to seek forgiveness.

Mohammed was obviously a Muslim, like most Egyptians. So before praying I told him I was going to talk again to God. Then I bowed my head and said, "Forgive me, Lord, for thinking only of myself. Help me to thank you for my blessings, and not to complain about my problems." Then I added this solemn promise: "Dear God, you saved my life. Today I give it back to you. I want to serve you any way I can. Amen."

After that, my physical condition didn't change right away, but my attitude did. Then one morning the door to my room swung open and I saw a familiar face. It was Dr. Fouad, our friend who took us to buy shoes. That's when I knew God had heard my prayers and things were going to work out just fine.

Dr. Fouad was accompanied that day by one of his colleagues, a famous surgeon named Dr. Mofed, known throughout the country and in other parts of the world for his medical expertise. He walked over to my bed and began to examine me. The frown on his face showed he was not pleased.

Suddenly the hospital physician charged into the room. "Who are you and what are you doing? You have no right to examine my patient."

Dr. Mofed was furious. "You say I can't examine the boy? Fine! Then I will take him to a private hospital, where he will receive the care he should have been getting here."

"You will not take him anywhere. I won't permit it. Who do you think you are, talking to me this way?"

"I am Dr. Mofed, and I don't need your permission to do anything!"

When the hospital physician heard the surgeon's name, his face turned white. "Forgive me, sir, I had no idea. I will release him to you at once." Then he ran from the room.

Before I knew what was happening, official forms had been signed and I was in Dr. Fouad's car on my way to a different hospital. Over the next month I had two major operations performed by Dr. Mofed and countless hours of therapy. It was a very difficult time, but at least I finally began to get better.

One fine day Dr. Fouad told Mama I was strong enough to go home. It felt so good to walk the streets of my neighborhood, see my friends, and be in my own home. Our two-room flat never looked so good, and Mama's care was better than any nurse's could ever be.

When I felt strong enough, I headed back to school. It had been three long months since that dark December day my family still refers to as Black Thursday, not Friday. I was far behind in all of my subjects: Arabic and mathematics, history and English grammar, and all the rest. For the next month I worked as hard as I knew how to catch up; but even with the help of my teachers, it didn't look good. When my final exams were only days away, I felt like giving up.

Mama went to talk to my teachers, and they all recommended I repeat my final year, then sit for the exams. When she told me what they said, I replied, "No, Mama, I'll take them now. At least I must try."

When my grades were posted, they were nine points below the minimum to qualify for secondary school. For first time in my academic life I had failed to measure up. That afternoon I stood outside the school and watched my friends jumping and shouting, "I made it! I made it!" My bus ride home was very lonely, and I couldn't even cry until I found a place where no one could see me.

Now there were only two possible choices: transfer to a private school with high tuition (which we couldn't afford), or repeat my final year at prep school. So I swallowed my pride and agreed to the second option. As it turned out, the year went quite well this time. My marks were some of the highest, and my final exam grades were excellent. This qualified me to move on to the next chapter of my life.

I was a bit apprehensive as my first secondary school term began. The next three years would be a challenge, and I didn't want to fail. At the same time, I knew God's plan for me was in some kind of ministry, and this gave me an indescribable peace.

Then one day while I was mulling over some of my boyhood dreams, out tumbled a statement that had once made me angry: *You are the man; you will replace your father.* Strangely, those words didn't upset me anymore. Instead, I began to wonder if they just might be true.

9

IN BABA'S FOOTSTEPS

1970–1990
CAIRO

My three years in secondary school saw big changes in me as the Lord began using my pain and suffering to mold me as a person. I was no longer a young boy thinking about only my own wants and needs. God started teaching me to reach out to those around me, looking for ways to serve them in any way possible. He continued to patiently smooth some of my rough edges, and as the leaders of our church began to see these changes, they invited me to teach the children's classes. Apparently my earlier impulsive behavior had been forgiven. Although I was still a teenager, God's hand of blessing was present in my teaching, and many of the children in my classes accepted the Lord as their Savior. It slowly became clear that I actually was starting to follow in Baba's footsteps.

As I grew spiritually, other responsibilities were added, such as visiting the sick and leading adult services. When the church launched monthly all-night prayer meetings, I put them on my agenda. We prayed from Thursday evening till Friday morning, and nothing could keep me from attending. There were times when I fell asleep while kneeling on the floor, only to wake up with people praying all around me. Still, no matter what other responsibilities I had, my main focus would always be on children.

In spite of the blessings that came to me through ministry, the rest of my life was much more stressful. I worked hard at my studies, knowing that top grades were required in order to get into the university. In addition to that, whenever I looked at Mama my heart would ache. No matter how hard she worked, it was never enough. Time and again that phrase, "You are the man," came to mind, and I felt guilty for not becoming the father in our family. Often these pressures brought me to tears.

Around the time of my fifteenth birthday, this burden of family responsibility became too heavy. As the oldest son I knew it was time to help Mama, so I went looking for a job. Near the bus stop was a wholesale strawberry business. Huge lorries collected fruit from farms and transported it to this warehouse, where it was resold to retailers. One afternoon

I bravely walked in the front door and asked to speak to the boss.

The company was owned by two businessmen, one old and one young. When I was taken to the older man, I stepped up to him and bravely said, "Sir, I wish to apply for a job."

The gentleman looked me up and down for several seconds and then replied, "Okay, young fellow, we will give you a try. You start tonight."

I was assigned to the night shift and given the job of weighing and pricing the strawberries. At the end of my shift they paid me a small commission. I felt so proud the first time I walked up to Mama and handed her my earnings.

In no time at all I found it was a bit tricky to work for two bosses. The older one was quite nice, but his young partner made me feel uneasy. And it wouldn't be long before my misgivings about him were confirmed. One night the old man fell from a tractor and broke his leg. When he was unable to return to work in the warehouse, he sent word he wanted to talk to me in his office. What he said really surprised me.

"Nathan, until my leg heals I am putting you in charge of our business. You will keep track of all the accounts and all of the money each day, then report back to me."

"I don't understand, sir. Why me and not your partner?"

"Because I cannot trust my partner."

When the owner insisted, of course I agreed.

The younger boss was quite upset when he found out about these new arrangements. A few nights later he came to me and said, "Nathan, let's make a deal. When you weigh the strawberries, instead of writing four kilos, make it three. You and I will pocket the difference, and the old man will never know." When I refused, he was furious.

Later that night I heard the rumble of a motor behind me. I whirled in time to see the young partner on a tractor headed straight for me. I leaped out of the way just before being crushed against a shipping crate. My heart was beating wildly as I ran to the office to tell my older boss what had just happened. He thanked me for being honest, sent for his partner, and demanded they dissolve their partnership immediately.

The old gentleman showed his appreciation for my honesty by keeping me employed throughout my secondary school years. My steady income helped provide for our family, and it made life much more pleasant for Mama. Once again, God was taking care of us.

When graduation time rolled around again, my secondary school grades qualified me to continue my studies at the university. Since not everyone was allowed to go to college in Egypt, it was another big milestone for me. Now it was time to decide on a major.

Ever since I was a small boy, Mama had always referred to me as Doctor-Nathan-this and Doctor-Nathan-that. After a while everyone started calling me Doctor Nathan, and I began to wonder if God might want me to become a physician. One evening I was at home trying to think through this matter when a young girl came running down the hall and into our flat. She was frantic, tugging at my arm, saying, "Doctor Nathan, come quick! Something is wrong with my father!"

As we raced down the street, I thought, *This girl looks familiar. Do I know her?* When we dashed into her house behind the grocery store, I got my answer. There on the floor was our kind neighborhood grocer. I dropped to my knees to try to help the man, but it didn't look good.

When the real doctor arrived, my worst fears were confirmed: our friend was gone. The man's family said there had been no warning. He simply walked from his grocery to the kitchen, picked up a cup of tea, and collapsed in a heap. Again the dark shadow of death had passed near me. I loved this kind man and would miss him dearly. But I knew from my own experiences that his wife and daughters would miss him much more.

On the way back to our flat, I wondered if this sad event had a deeper meaning. I finally concluded that in our lifetime we were to care for those around us, as this man had. Then when our work is finished, the Lord would call us home. Again, I thought, *Maybe God does want me to be a doctor.*

When university enrollment time came, though, I went in a slightly different direction. Instead of becoming a "people doctor," I was led by the Lord to a program in veterinary medicine. I loved animals, and it soon became clear this was God's path for me for now. In a city like Cairo, there were plenty of goats, donkeys, dogs, and cats to keep me busy. Mama was so proud. Soon her Nathan would really be a doctor.

Unfortunately, other people did not share Mama's feelings. Pastors and church leaders began bombarding me with advice. "You must go to Bible school," they insisted. "You are gifted, and you would be a great pastor." The pressure from these well-meaning friends and mentors was almost unbearable at times, but I was convinced God was not leading me in that direction. So I enrolled in the veterinary program, thinking this would likely be a temporary vocation. I knew, in the Lord's good time, he would reveal his perfect will for my life.

The five years I spent at the university were consumed by an intensive and difficult course load, and it was made even harder by one unexpected challenge. Many of my professors were Muslims, and once they discovered I was a Christian they began treating me differently from the rest of my classmates. By the time I appeared for my oral exams at the end of the first year I expected the worst.

On the day of the test my entire class assembled outside the examining rooms, where we all sat waiting nervously. When it was our turn, we were called in groups of three to be questioned by one of our professors. My pulse was racing as I walked into the next room with two Muslim classmates. My heart sank as I saw who was waiting there. Sitting behind the desk was a man known for being extremely anti-Christian. After asking the two Muslim students a series of quite simple questions about animal anatomy, the professor smiled warmly and said, "Excellent answers. I have nothing further to ask. You are excused." When the door closed, he turned to me.

"Well, Nathan, now it is your turn. Come over here and take a look at these jars. I want you to examine them carefully." After a short pause he said, "The jars contain the organs of a cow, a camel, and a water buffalo. I want you to tell me which is which, and how you can tell the difference."

I thought, *I can't believe this is happening.* There was no possible way to answer correctly by simply looking at the specimens. When I had no answer, the professor flashed an evil smile and sarcastically said, "You don't know? Then I must give you a failing grade. You may leave."

Because of this experience I was required to re-take my exam three months later, but this time I appeared before a different professor and earned a very high score. It wasn't the first time I faced such unfair treatment, and it was not the last. It is the price Christian students often paid at most universities in Egypt.

After graduation I launched my career as a veterinarian, caring for animals of all kinds in communities on the outskirts of Cairo. It was very enjoyable work, paid quite well, and enabled me to help support my family. My reputation was given a real boost when I treated the dearly loved pet of a prominent businessman. I correctly diagnosed the cause of the dog's problem and cured it, and when word of my treatment spread I suddenly became rather well-known.

When my three sisters married and my brother Magdy left for Bible school, our little flat was not so crowded any more. After he graduated in 1982 Magdy pastored for a while, then decided to establish an organization focused on discipling young men for ministry. It was the first of its kind in Egypt. I became involved as a volunteer, while at the same time maintaining my veterinary practice. Those were busy days, but since I was single it didn't really bother me.

In the summer of 1986 a visiting professor from New Zealand Bible College came to lecture in Cairo. He was an excellent teacher, and he also spent countless hours advising me on finding God's direction for my life. At the conclusion of the course he offered me a one-year scholarship at his school, which I immediately accepted. The following January I boarded a plane bound for the distant city of Christchurch.

When I landed in New Zealand, everything looked new. There were vast, green fields with huge flocks of sheep and orderly rows of individual houses with bright, colorful flowers. I saw paved streets and fancy cars, blue lakes and bubbling streams—and the people! I couldn't believe how warm and friendly they were. It seemed like heaven, compared to life back in Egypt.

One of my classes at the Bible college radically changed my entire view of the Christian walk. It was called "Which Way to Righteousness: Grace or Law?" It opened my eyes to a brand-new understanding of God's grace. Although I considered myself a good Christian, I really wasn't enjoying my Christianity. This class completely reshaped my thinking in this area, and it altered both my personal walk with God and the way I approached ministry.

I did encounter one unexpected challenge not directly related to my studies. I met a nice New Zealand girl, and for a time I considered marrying her and ministering in that beautiful land. Then I thought, *No, this is not why you came here, Nathan. You belong back in Egypt.* For the first time I came face-to-face with the central purpose of my life: to serve God among my own people.

After returning to Cairo I didn't return to my veterinary practice. Instead, I began working full-time with Magdy, discipling a new generation of Christian leaders. Now I was not only more qualified than I had been but also more understanding of those around me, and—best of all—more understanding of God's grace that could completely change their lives.

As our work continued to grow, we found we had a serious problem. Due to a shortage of teachers, we could not enroll all our applicants in formal classes. We didn't want to turn anyone away, so we launched a series of Bible correspondence courses. The news of these lessons spread like wildfire, and in no time students from across the country were signing up.

It wasn't long before we heard reports of others using our materials. In one of our large cities, a local pastor organized a conference on prayer. The man was having a hard time holding the attention of his audience until someone brought him a colorful brochure on the topic. "We just received this in the mail," they said. "Why don't you give it a try?" It energized his lectures, and after the conference he was besieged by people asking, "Where can we get this literature?" It was one of our lessons.

We also introduced another unique outreach: a course on reconciliation between Jews and Christians. Bear in mind that for many centuries there has been nothing but war and violence between Egypt and Israel. All we ever heard in our schools and news media were words of hatred and calls for revenge aimed at these neighbors. Travel was even prohibited between our two countries until the Camp David Peace Treaty was signed in 1979. This meant that in the 1980s any kind of contact with Jews was still a revolutionary idea.

In 1981, Magdy managed to travel to Israel by going first to Cyprus. His goal was to minister to Arabic people in northern Israel. We had assumed that there were no Christians in that region, but much to Magdy's surprise he found many Messianic Jews, and they extended a warm welcome to him. This established a bridge of fellowship between believers in our two countries.

After a few more such visits, we decided the next step was to bring Jewish Christians to our country. So in 1986 we organized an event in Alexandria. For the first time in recent history, believers from Israel joined with Egyptian Christians in worship. We celebrated the true peace that comes only from the Prince of Peace, Jesus Christ. It was a foretaste of heaven to see over two hundred Jesus followers praising God in both Hebrew and Arabic, all at the same time.

As God poured ever-increasing blessings on our ministry, we realized we could not keep operating like a small village church. Formal organization was necessary if we hoped to survive. In our region, this was often accomplished by way of a school. So after much prayer and many long talks, we decided to move in that direction.

We immediately faced a whole new set of challenges. We had to find a building, secure funding, fill out reams of governmental paperwork—the list went on and on. There were times when our dream seemed unattainable and we were tempted to give up. But in September 1990, after two hectic years of work, we were licensed to enroll our first class of students.

Each year we added another grade, until the school included kindergarten through grade nine. Our enrollment increased to over three hundred and fifty of the brightest boys and girls in Cairo, and our academic reputation also continued to grow until we were recognized as the best school in our district.

Each year there seemed to be an ever-increasing number of Muslim children applying for admission. We conducted pre-enrollment interviews with the parents, being careful to explain that this was a Christian school and that our teaching was based on biblical principles. We wanted to avoid any possible misunderstandings later.

One day a father in a snow-white *galabayya* walked into my office followed by his wife, who was wrapped from head to toe in the traditional long black Arabic *burka*. They wanted to enroll their five-year-old for the fall term. After we explained how our school was operated, he responded with these clear and kind words: "We understand your school is operated according to the best educational standards and highest moral values, and that is what we want for our son. I know you will teach him well, and you will also teach us how to raise our children to a good life."

This kind of affirmation was not something we actively sought, but it did confirm that God's hand was on our ministry. We continued to face new challenges, but we also saw the Lord's blessings day by day. As for me personally, the biggest blessing of all was to be ministering to children, just like Baba.

10

WHO IS SHE?

JUNE 1988–SEPTEMBER 1989
CAIRO AND ASYUT

After I graduated from the university, Mama decided it was time for me to take a wife. The topic of marriage didn't interest me at all; there was far too much going on in my life at that time. However, this didn't stop Mama. She constantly tried to match me up with first one and then another eligible prospect, usually from our little church.

"What is wrong with you, Nathan? When will you marry? I want to hold my grandsons," she would say. I would simply smile, give her one of those "Someday, Mama" answers, then go on about my business. These little conversations continued for quite some time, until a surprise encounter suddenly changed my outlook.

In June 1988, Magdy and I decided to organize a national teaching seminar for young adults. We reserved a conference center in Ismailia, a large city to the east of Cairo near the Suez Canal, then mailed invitations to young people throughout the country. Soon we were flooded with registration requests, far beyond our wildest expectations. The greatest response came from the south, which made me so happy, since that's where we used to live. We quickly put plans in motion to make this a life-changing event.

Many of the students came to the conference by train, so I went to the station to meet them. There was a strange mixture of expressions on their faces as they climbed down from their coaches. Some seemed right at home, while others looked like frightened children looking for a place to hide. I thought, *First time in Cairo? I know just how you feel.*

By this time I had reached the ripe old age of thirty-two, and to these young adults I was regarded as something of a Bible scholar. So I was thinking through my opening lecture, not wanting to disappoint them—and that's when I saw her. She had long, dark hair, a radiant smile, and was stunningly beautiful. But the feature that absolutely captured me was her eyes. They sparkled and danced with so much life I couldn't turn away. Without thinking, I actually said, "Who is she?" The sound of my voice startled me and I took a nervous look around, hoping no one had heard. Then I whispered to myself, "What's going on, Nathan? You've never felt this way before."

When the last of the students arrived, we herded everyone onto our rented bus and set out for the conference center. There were lots of "oohs" and "ahs" along the way as first-time visitors to Cairo took in the sights and sounds outside: the honking horns, the tall buildings, and the hordes of people. Meanwhile, I was busy looking around inside the bus, trying to locate that face again. She had to be onboard, but no matter where I looked she didn't seem to be there. It was as if she had simply evaporated.

A team of volunteers was waiting to register the participants when we arrived in Ismailia. Then everyone gathered in the conference hall for my opening address. It was almost impossible for me to teach my lessons that day. All I wanted to do was find a certain face. I finally located her in the back of the hall, chatting happily with several friends.

Usually whenever I taught or preached I was quite focused, but not that day. In each session my mind was divided into two parts, one for teaching and the other for impressing someone. Even though her name was still a mystery, I thought, *No problem. I'll introduce myself at the end of my evening lecture.* But it didn't happen. Before I could catch her, she had gone to her room. So much for day one.

The second day definitely called for a different approach, so I divided the conferees into eight small groups, each with its own leader. After discovering the mystery girl's name was

Susan, I added her name to the leader list and posted it on the bulletin board. Then I announced, "All group leaders are to meet with me in the dining room." Now she was one of only eight, much closer to my ultimate goal. Meanwhile, this Susan-whom-I-did-not-know wondered why she had been picked to lead. She didn't feel qualified, and it was probably for the best that she didn't know the real reason.

For the rest of the conference I tried my best to catch Susan's eye, but with no success. In Egypt it's improper for young ladies to show interest in men they don't know, so in spite of my most brilliant strategies I might as well have been pouring water on desert sand. By the end of the week my Susan-with-the-captivating-eyes did not seem the least bit curious about me.

On the last day of the conference I accidentally overheard a most interesting conversation. Susan's group was staying in Cairo for a few extra days. Suddenly I remembered that the youth leader from Asyut was a distant cousin of mine. That's when a voice seemed to say, *Wake up, Nathan. What took you so long?* It was time to have a chat with my cousin.

"There is a girl named Susan from your region. What can you tell me about her?" I asked him. He actually knew her quite well, so he filled me in on her family background, her walk with the Lord, and many other details. Then he added one more significant tidbit: she was not yet engaged.

When he finished I said, "I must meet her. Will you help me?"

He shot me one of those sly, all-knowing grins and laid out a plan. Right then I would have agreed to anything.

"Tomorrow night we are going to the amusement park," he said. "Why don't you 'accidentally' show up, and we'll see what happens."

Since Mama was still pushing me to marry, there was no way I was going to mention Susan to her yet. She would have jumped right in and tried to move things along. Dear Mama. Her intentions were above reproach, but her methods sometimes left a bit to be desired. So the next evening I dressed in my best clothes, slipped out of our flat, and headed for the amusement park.

The young people were genuinely surprised to see me stroll up and ask to join their group. They enthusiastically agreed, and I tried to show an equal amount of enthusiasm, while keeping my eye on a certain girl named Susan. Later, when it came time for Ferris wheel rides, my cousin declared, "No one can ride until I say so." Each car held only two passengers, and it was no accident when he called out, "Nathan and Susan!" Her name was like music in my ears.

Before I knew it, I was floating through the air with this beautiful angel, alone in our own little world. My heart was beating wildly and I wondered what Susan was thinking. Did she approve of my actions? Sitting in that swinging seat, all I could do was stare at her. Finally, she slowly turned her big dark eyes toward me and smiled. My memory is a bit fuzzy after that, but you can be sure of one thing: Susan and I had a fantastic evening together, and it would not be our last. On my way home I thought, *Cousin, I will be indebted to you forever.*

Dating customs for young people in Egypt were much different than those in Western countries, and courtship rules in 1988 had not changed much since the days of Latif and Hyat. Some people would say we stretched them quite a bit that evening, but that thought never even entered my head.

In any event, when his youth group returned home, my cousin went immediately to Susan's family to tell them about a certain man named Nathan. It was like a lightning bolt from the sky. They promptly started firing questions, and the first was, "Who is he?" Then they bombarded my poor cousin with a whole list of queries: "What, you say he's a city boy? You think he wants to marry Susan? Is he a good man? Who are his parents? We need to know a lot more. Who can we talk to?" No stranger was about to come marching into Asyut and carry away their dear Susan, and certainly not one from Cairo.

Upon hearing of their reaction, we quickly sent a message to the family requesting a formal visit. Susan's family story was very similar to mine. Her father had died a few years earlier, and her oldest brother, Nabil, was now head of the family. He agreed to receive us, so at the appointed hour Mama, Magdy, and I arrived at their home. When we got inside, Susan was nowhere to be seen.

Over cups of black tea we went through the same ceremonial conversations that had taken place between the families

116

of my father and mother. It was as if we were reading from a script. When we finished, Nabil asked for time to consider our proposal and promised to send word soon of their decision. I wasn't too optimistic when we headed back to Cairo. Susan's mother hadn't looked at all happy. After all, it was the first time her daughter had attended any kind of conference, and now look what had happened.

After we left, Susan's relatives launched their own investigation. They went to see the pastor, who gave them a good report of our family. Several of their friends also knew us, and they added positive words. Then the matter was discussed at great length by her entire family.

Finally, one evening at dinner Nabil turned to Susan and said, "Sister, I hear about a man from Cairo named Nathan. Do you know him?" He already knew the answer.

"Yes, my brother, I know him."

After a short pause, he continued.

"We hear he is a good man. And what do you say about him, Susan?"

"I have heard the same." This was no time to mention rides on a Ferris wheel.

Her mother gently injected, "Tell me, Susan, is he a godly man?"

"Of course, Mama, or we wouldn't be talking this way."

Then her brother posed the big question. "All right, now that we know who Nathan is, and have been told many good things about him, I have only one more question." He paused a little longer, then asked, "Sister, are you sure you want to marry him?"

Before answering, Susan looked around the room at each member of her family. Then she softly said, "Nabil, I have been fasting and praying for days; but I need a bit more time to be sure. For now, though, I believe the answer will be yes."

After agreeing to talk again soon, the conversation ended.

Susan didn't want to rush her decision, and it seemed God was not in a hurry either. But Mama was so excited she couldn't stop calling to see what Susan's reply would be. Apparently, she liked Susan from the first day they met, because Susan was also studying to be a doctor (doctor of pharmacology, that is) just like me.

The pressure began to build at Susan's house. After a few more days of prayer, she knew it was time to decide. Would it be yes, or would it be no? Then one morning a peace filled her heart that could only come from the Lord, and she knew marrying me was the right thing to do. That evening at dinner she shared her decision with Nabil and the rest of the family.

Nabil quickly phoned me in Cairo and said, "We would like you to come again, as soon as possible." I knew this was a good sign, and we agreed on the following Friday, a day when Nabil would not be working. It was the first of many good Fridays that would help me forget that really bad one.

Magdy again made the trip with me to act as mediator, and naturally Mama came as well. As soon as we arrived we all sat down for a wonderful meal, but everyone knew we had not driven seven hours just to have dinner. So after Susan's mother served tea, it was time to talk business.

There we all sat: Magdy, Mama, and I were on one side of the room and Susan, Nabil, and their mother were on the other. Neither Susan nor I said a word. The discussions would be carried out between our brothers. But of course both mamas inserted their thoughts several times.

The conversation followed the usual pattern that our culture had observed for centuries. After all of the proper questions had been answered, Nabil turned to Susan and said, "We will now select a date for the engagement ceremony. The other matters you and I will talk about later." And we all knew, then, that Susan's brother had decided to approve the proposal, and the discussions were finished.

Once the date had been agreed to, we gathered in a circle and Magdy offered a prayer of thanksgiving. "Oh Lord, we thank you for bringing this couple together, and today we place them in your hands. We pray that you will guide them, guard them, and bless the home they are about to establish. Amen."

This time when we left Susan's house, I was quite happy. As Magdy drove us back to Cairo, I started making a list of things that had to be done. I needed to select a pastor to perform the engagement ceremony and a music leader for the event, to invite family members who would attend, and to coordinate their travel to the south. Worst of all, I would have to buy myself a new suit. I hated wearing suits, but I knew Mama would insist.

As our engagement day approached, we prepared to return to Asyut. Onsey and my sisters traveled with Mama by train, while Magdy and I picked up the pastor, worship leader, and two other friends. The only route to Asyut was a dusty, unpaved farm road and our van was not air-conditioned, so it was like traveling in a four-wheeled oven.

Magdy again did the driving, so I let my mind drift to the engagement activities. I envisioned a perfect evening with a perfect girl, with nothing going wrong. Then just as we rolled into a small village, a motorcycle suddenly shot across the road in front of us. Magdy jammed on the brakes, but he couldn't stop in time. The motorcycle flew in one direction while the man cartwheeled through the air, smashed into our windshield, and slid to the ground. We were quickly surrounded by a mob of screaming people.

"The man is not moving, he's dead!"

"What kind of driver are you?"

"Crazy people from Cairo!"

"Grab the driver, don't let him get away!"

A village policeman came running down the street and immediately took charge. Otherwise, I'm not sure what would have happened.

An ambulance rushed the motorcyclist to a clinic and the officer took us to the police station. Since Magdy was driving, he was locked in a room by himself; the rest of us were left outside, not knowing what to do. Meanwhile, Mama and the other guests had arrived in Asyut and were expecting us to meet their train. There were no phones in the village and no way to get a message to them, and the longer they waited, the more concerned they became.

Back in the village, the policeman launched a spirited investigation. He contacted the clinic to check on the man; he questioned Magdy over and over; he called for witnesses to the accident; he phoned the license bureau. The officer was having a wonderful time, but I was not. My dream of a perfect engagement had been destroyed in a flash.

At last the policeman concluded that the motorcyclist had no license, was clearly at fault in the accident, and would recover from his injuries. We were told we could leave, but the officer wouldn't release our van. He claimed it had to be "checked for mechanical issues." He even locked up our luggage, musical instruments, and my new suit.

After much pleading, we were allowed to reclaim our belongings, and then we hired a car and driver to take us on to Asyut. When we arrived, we found my family in a state of panic. They were relieved that we were all right, but judging by Mama's behavior, you wouldn't think so. She acted like the accident had been all Magdy's fault.

After a short night's rest, everyone gathered at Susan's church for the engagement service. There were no unexpected interruptions, and the day was almost as perfect as I had dreamed it would be. Then, in traditional Egyptian fashion, the occasion was capped off with a sumptuous feast of roast chicken, fresh vegetables seasoned with leeks and garlic, and other tasty favorites.

―――――――

The next year was a special time for Susan and me. For Christian couples in Egypt, engagement is more than a get-acquainted period. It is a time when they wait for God to affirm the lifetime commitment they are about to make. As for Susan and me, the more time we spent together, the more certain we were that our decision to marry was right.

Over the next several months I traveled to the south about every two weeks to see Susan. During that time God gave me many opportunities to minister in churches. I also started several Bible studies focused on spreading the gospel to places where it was not known. Then I organized and trained evangelistic teams to minister in villages near Asyut where there were no churches. Without my knowing it, the Lord was planting seeds for my future ministry.

Susan and I both have wonderful memories of our courtship year, but it was also quite hard in some ways. While the majority of Egypt's evangelical Christians were located in the south, the region had also been a stronghold for many radical Islamic groups for the past century. When my father was killed their influence and actions impacted every area of life, and this was still true during my engagement over twenty-five years later.

As Susan was completing her last year of pharmacy school, I stopped by her university one day. She had to walk from one building to another between classes, and I thought we could make the stroll together. It didn't occur to me that we needed a chaperone.

There was a soft drink shop along the street, so we stopped to have a cola. As we stood outside sipping our soda, we noticed four tall, angry-looking men close by. Their shaggy beards and dark *galabayyas* clearly identified them as members of a radical Muslim group. It was obvious they were watching us, and without a word they signaled me to come to them.

"Do as they say," Susan whispered. "If you don't, they will do something bad to us."

I walked to them and they immediately surrounded me. I looked up into their dark faces, and I could almost smell the anger.

One man was obviously their leader, and he hissed, "Who is she?"

"Susan is my fiancée, and I have come to visit her."

"Don't you know you are not to be alone with each other? Our scriptures clearly teach that when an unmarried man and woman are together, the devil is there too."

"This is a new teaching to me. I am a Christian from Cairo, and I have no desire to offend you or your teachings."

The man paused for a minute, then spoke again. "We will excuse you this time. But if we see you together this way in the future, we will kill you. Now go, both of you, in different directions. And remember, never again."

Without saying a word, both of us started walking, Susan to her class and me away from the university. We never forgot that day, and for the rest of the year we carefully avoided making the same mistake again.

In June 1989 Susan received her pharmacy degree, and we were married in September. Our wedding was much like the marriage of Latif and Hyat, but without the camel. There had been a few changes in Egypt since my parents were married. It was such a blessing to finally have Susan alongside me. There may be only one other person who enjoyed welcoming her into our family as much as I did. It was Mama.

11

BUMPS IN THE ROAD

1989–1995
CAIRO AND BEYOND

September 1989 was the beginning of a wonderful chapter in my life. By that time Onsey had settled in London following his university years, so Mama and I had been living quite comfortably in the same little two-room flat that had been our home since moving to Cairo. We really didn't need anything larger. But after the wedding Susan and I quickly found a place of our own, as you would expect.

As for me, the word "new" again described my life. I had a new wife, a new home, and new ministries. I also had a brand-new school about to open, with a long list of responsibilities. Those were very busy times.

The first months of marriage were happy and peaceful for Susan and me. But there was one somewhat painful adjustment that came to our family. I didn't realize it at first, but when I moved to my own home with Susan, it was a difficult time for Mama. Until then she had looked to me as her man in the family, and for several years I handled all of the husbandly chores around our flat. That quickly ended when I moved out, and soon I began to see a gradual change in Mama's attitude toward Susan. This caught me completely by surprise, and at first I couldn't figure out what was wrong.

When I mentioned this change to Susan, she agreed that something was not quite right. Before long it became clear to me that Mama's problem was about more than just household matters. Although she had been pressing me to marry, it was easy to understand how she felt now that another woman had "taken her Nathan." If it were not for Susan's tender and sensitive spirit, this could have been a tough time for all of us. Instead, I watched my wife lovingly show Mama that she had no desire to *take* Nathan, she only wanted to *share* him. And today, nearly twenty-five years later, they are still happily sharing me.

Once this matter was settled, Mama could have become quiet and contented; but no, she simply turned her attention to a new topic. She wanted a grandson, and she didn't want to wait forever. In addition to *her* prodding, Susan's family was doing the same. My wife was one of six girls with only one brother, so adding a boy to their family was a high priority too.

To be honest, the fatherhood business didn't concern me as much as it did everyone else. It would happen in due time, I figured. Besides, I had been the acting father for my brothers and sisters when they were younger. Helping Magdy and Onsey with their homework and other manly things had actually been enjoyable, and at times I had even taken care of parental discipline when I felt it was necessary. So the job of being a "real parent" now that I was married didn't seem to be all that difficult.

I must admit, though, sometimes my parenting efforts had not been well received by my brothers. Like normal boys, they would head outside after school to play with the neighbor kids. The street was their only playground, and there was always a game of soccer or cricket going on. Often the intense rivalries led to angry confrontations. That's when I would spoil their fun by ordering them inside to do homework and household chores. They would grudgingly obey, only to slip off later to watch TV at a friend's house.

As for my sisters, Mama taught them about housekeeping, cooking, and such things. But their big family issues fell on my shoulders. When young men came to call, they would ask, "Where is the father?" I would respond, "I am the father. You must deal with me." Later I would talk to my sisters about these things, but final decisions regarding their relationships were left to me.

In spite of these parental practice experiences, I soon discovered how different life can be when you have children of your own. One day when I came home from the office, Susan met me at the door and greeted me with a familiar phrase.

"Nathan, we need to talk."

With a chuckle, I said, "I thought so. What is it?"

She replied in a hesitant whisper, "I think I'm . . . pregnant."

"You what?! What do you mean 'I think'? Are you sure?"

"Well, pretty sure. The doctor did a test, and it came back positive."

I began jumping up and down, then grabbed Susan and started whirling her around our flat. Then it occurred to me that my wife shouldn't be so reckless in her condition and we collapsed on the couch in each other's arms. So much for not being interested in parenting. We couldn't wait to call our mamas.

Unlike our parents, we didn't need to wait until the baby arrived to find out if our child was a boy or girl. Our doctor could simply perform a sonogram, so we rang his office at once to make the arrangements. On the appointed day, the doctor took Susan into an examining room, leaving me to pace about the waiting area.

After what seemed like an eternity, the door opened and Susan appeared. As is often the case when she is nervous, Susan couldn't look me in the eye. She just walked over to a couch, sat down, and started playing with the wrinkles in her dress.

It seemed that my wife had lost her voice. Finally my patience ran out and I said, "Don't just sit there, Susan. What did the doctor say?"

A tiny tear began to trickle down her cheek. Without looking up, she replied, "I'm so sorry, Nathan. It's . . . a girl."

"A girl? Really, is that what the doctor said?"

"I'm not joking, Nathan. We will have a baby girl."

There is no denying that we were disappointed for a while. In fact, for the first time I could understand how Baba must have felt so many years before. But once little Maggie moved into our lives, those feelings of disappointment quickly evaporated. Her bright, happy smile captured our hearts from the day she arrived, and she has been a blessing from God ever since. She has grown up to become a real help to her mother at home and an indispensable part of our ministry. There is no question that Maggie was the perfect firstborn for Susan and me.

At the same time, our families were not at all satisfied. They still wanted a boy who would carry on the family name, and the level of urgency in our generation was greater than in my parents' day. Back then it was quite common to see families with six or seven or more children. But by the time we became parents, providing for even two or three was difficult, since it was becoming hard to scratch out a living. The transition from agricultural to urban life was impacting Egypt, and our economy was beginning to crumble.

Before Maggie reached her first birthday, Susan happily announced that she was expecting our second child. Again we visited the doctor for a sonogram, and again our families sat glued to their telephones awaiting the news, especially Mama. I was afraid if we had another girl, she might banish me from her presence forever.

After thirty nerve-wracking minutes, the door opened and Susan reappeared. This time as she ran across the room, a huge smile accompanied her tears. All she said to me was, "Yes! Yes! Yes!" I kept asking, "Are you sure, are you sure, really sure?"

When we finally settled down, I dashed to the public phone and called Mama. I can still recall her joyful screams. Then she told me to get off the line so she could spread the news. In no time, everyone had heard her proudly proclaim, "Nathan and Susan will have a baby boy!"

When our second little one arrived we named him Martin, partly because of my studies of Martin Luther. Susan and I could not have been happier. Life was going exactly according to plan, and we could now focus our attention on ministry.

As we watched Maggie and Martin grow, our ministry was also increasing. God gave me a vision to train Christian workers and leaders, teaching them the basics of the faith, training teams of believers in evangelism, and sending them to spread the gospel in villages all across the south. Since our day school was in Cairo we continued to live there, but our work now reached far beyond the city.

We were again reminded that a growing ministry experiences growing pains. One challenge we felt compelled to tackle was the lack of cooperation and fellowship between believers from multiple denominations. Many attempts had been made in the past to bring these groups together, but with little success.

After much prayer and planning, we began a campaign to break down the invisible barriers that seemed to separate us. We avoided narrow, divisive topics and centered our teaching on clearly defined biblical doctrines. Then we waited to see what the Lord would do. Soon we saw Methodists, Baptists, Presbyterians, Assemblies of God, Catholics, and Coptics all gathering together to study God's Word and praise his name. This fellowship and interaction between believers only came about through the power of the Holy Spirit.

As a result of our growing outreach, the correspondence courses we had introduced earlier became an even greater tool. Enrollment increased to over three thousand students, many from outside the country. It would have been physically impossible to respond to such a widespread demand for Bible teaching without these lessons. They also provided a degree of protection for people who felt uncomfortable studying in traditional open classes.

Alongside these blessings, I must tell you about a dark and sinister shadow that began to hover over our lives. By way of an anonymous phone call, we discovered we were being watched by the authorities. It seems that when organizations like ours begin to grow, they pose a threat to the government, especially when the group is connected to anything Christian.

We began receiving mysterious phone calls from unidentified officials inviting me to their office to discuss some "serious matters." Usually I was told to come immediately; no further explanation was given, and refusing to appear was not an option. When I arrived, they would search me, take my personal identity card and any valuables, then leave me locked in an empty room for hours—sometimes till after midnight.

Finally I would be taken to a high official, who would offer a false apology with a fake smile then force me to remain standing for my entire interview. He would open my file and begin to fire innocent-sounding questions at me, things like:

"Where were you on such-and-such a date?"

"Why were you there, and who was with you?"

"What did you talk about, and did you say anything bad about the government?"

"Have you been back there since or met with these people anywhere else?"

Throughout the interview the officer would continually take notes. When he had heard enough, he would slap my file shut on his desk, flash another icy smile, and thank me for my cooperation. With a wave of his hand he would indicate I was dismissed. I would turn and walk from the room, often feeling wobbly from the long hours without food or water and from standing so long. After retrieving my valuables, I would make my way back home.

There was no way to predict when these calls would come. The phone would often ring in the wee hours of the night, and after the caller hung up I would hold Susan in my arms while she cried out her fears. I was frightened too, but I couldn't let her see it. After all, husbands aren't supposed to be afraid.

During one of these intense interviews, the authorities informed me that all of our teaching materials needed to be approved before they could be used in any schools or churches. Again it was made clear there was no choice. I soon discovered this irritating process could drag on for weeks, maybe even months.

These encounters became more frequent and more disturbing, and the pressure in our home continued to build. No clear charges or specific threats were ever made, but many frightening consequences were implied if we didn't cooperate. We knew of several friends who had suffered brutal beatings, while others were imprisoned for days or weeks, sometimes longer. Susan and I often went to bed at night wondering if I might be next. My heart ached when I saw the worry wrinkles in Susan's face, and I began to ask God, "What is going on, Lord? Is my life going to end like Baba's? This really isn't fair—not for me, and certainly not for my family."

As weeks turned into months, the stress began getting to me and I started to wonder, *How much more of this can we take, Lord? Look at what this is doing to Susan. Nearly every day something terrible happens.* Our situation kept going downhill, until one day I thought, *This is one hopeless mess, and there's no way to fix it. Perhaps our friends and relatives are right. Maybe it's time to get out of Egypt.*

12

RUNNING AWAY

While Susan and I were wrestling with the question of whether or not to flee our homeland, some very unsettling things were happening around us. From time to time, Christian friends would simply disappear. No one would say anything about where they went or why; we just didn't see them anymore.

At times like that it was easy to start imagining all sorts of scenes, none of them good. Did they move back to their old village? *Don't be silly; they would have told us goodbye.* Maybe they were taken by the authorities. *No, we would have heard about that.* In the end, after asking enough questions, we often discovered they had left the country.

These disappearances only added to the ongoing trauma and uncertainty in our lives. Then one day on her way home from work, Susan passed by the Canadian embassy. She saw several people clustered around a sign posted near the entrance, and out of curiosity she went over to check it out. What she read immediately captured her attention. It said:

WANTED: PHARMACISTS
Come to Canada . . . Jobs Waiting
Good Salaries . . . Good Schools
Applications Available from the Embassy
We Are Waiting to Welcome You!

Susan came bursting into our flat a few minutes later while I was working on a new correspondence lesson. One look at my wife told me she had something on her mind.

"Nathan, I just made the most amazing discovery. We must talk." After digging some sweets from her purse for Maggie and Martin, she sent them off to play in their room. To be honest, I really wasn't all that interested in hearing about another of my wife's discoveries right at that moment. But I patiently laid aside my work and waited to be amazed.

Susan came and sat by me on the couch, her eyes sparkling like two black diamonds. "As I was coming home I passed the Canadian embassy, which is not my usual way. You won't believe what I saw. Outside the main entrance was a big sign that said, 'Wanted, pharmacists. Come to Canada, jobs waiting.' It seemed like a dream, but I knew it wasn't. What do you think, Nathan? Maybe it is a message from God."

"What do I think? I think you're dreaming. It's probably only a coincidence."

"Nathan, don't you see? It's not a coincidence. I usually don't walk past the embassy; I take another street. But today it was closed for repairs. This was no accident, Nathan. Please, I think we should apply." Then she stopped and waited for me to answer.

There are times when it's best not to make some grand, prophetic proclamation, and this was one of them. I knew this had to be one of those too-good-to-be-true moments, but I also thought, *What can it hurt to apply?* So I tried to play it safe and see what would happen.

"Okay, Susan, if you want to fill out an application, go ahead. But don't get your hopes up. No doubt there is a long list of applicants, and we will never hear back from them."

Wrong again. A few weeks later our phone rang. When I picked it up, a North American–sounding lady said, "I am calling from the Office of Immigration at the Canadian embassy. We understand your wife is a pharmacist, and today we have been going over your application to move to Canada."

I thought, *Now I'm the one who is dreaming.* Without waiting for me to respond, she continued. "Our immigration director would like you and your wife to come for an interview next Tuesday at ten o'clock. Please bring your children with you."

I'm not quite sure how the rest of our conversation went. But whatever I said must have been all right, because the following Tuesday we found ourselves seated in an office at the embassy. Across the big, impressive desk was one of the friendliest men I have ever met. We were surprised when he told us his name was Mr. Martin, the same name as our son's. That's when I began to think perhaps Susan was right after all. Maybe this was a message from God.

We spent more than an hour talking with the director, while Maggie and Martin sat across the room, as quiet as two church mice. Not once did we feel like we were being formally interviewed. It was more like a casual conversation between friends. Mr. Martin wanted to hear about our children and our families, then our educational and professional training and experience.

When Mr. Martin seemed to run out of questions, he paused and began tapping the tips of his fingers together. Then he stood, walked around his desk, and shook hands with both of us. He said, "I don't think there is any reason to delay my answer to you. As of today, I promise your application will be approved. The only thing left is to arrange for physical examinations with our doctor. He will advise my office of the results. If he gives you a good report, and I'm sure he will, you will soon be on your way to Canada. Congratulations."

When I heard those words, a shiver ran down my spine and a big smile spread across Susan's face. Canada! It was a place where many Egyptians dreamed of living. I knew there would be this tiny problem of telling Mama we were leaving, but we wouldn't be the first ones to go. My sister Hoda had already moved to Vancouver, and soon it seemed we would join her there.

The next several days became a frantic race against the clock as we secured visas, made flight reservations, and completed an endless array of government documents. But the most important task of all was reorganizing the school staff to function smoothly without us. We were not about to allow six years of hard work to go down the drain. And in the few tiny gaps in our daily schedules, we began to feverishly pack our bags. One thing I asked Mama to keep for me was Baba's walking staff. I wasn't going to risk having it taken from me at the airport.

The long flight from Cairo to Vancouver reminded me of my trip to New Zealand, except for a couple of details. First, Susan was beside me this time, and second, we had two tired and irritable children with us. The excitement of their first airplane ride soon wore off and they went to sleep. When they woke up, we spent the rest of our time in a lot of game-playing and other distractions. Our plane finally landed in Vancouver and we slowly inched our way through the long customs lines. When we walked out of the arrivals hall, we were astonished to see a large group of family and friends waving hand-painted signs and carrying flowers for Susan. It was only the beginning of an extended reception welcoming us to our new home.

Just like when my family moved to Cairo, there was a flat waiting for us, with basic furniture and other necessities. As we unpacked, a neighbor even came to offer us a red leather couch, which we gladly accepted. Once we had found a spot for everything, we turned off the lights and crawled into bed.

Maggie and Martin quickly fell in love with that red couch. They would bounce up and down on the cushions until we made them stop. Then they would turn on the television and watch cartoons. Those early days in Vancouver seemed like heaven to us. There were no street demonstrations, no threatening phone calls, and no fears for the safety of our family. Now we had nice food, a nice, safe park nearby where the children could play, plus a fantastic school for Maggie that had rows of shiny desks and the latest books and equipment. After completing a few pharmacy classes to meet government requirements, Susan would soon be starting her new job. Our future looked fantastic, and we began to feel right at home in our new nest.

Then, one morning not long after we arrived, I started to hear a familiar sound. No one else was in the house that day. Susan was attending a class, Maggie was at school, and Martin had gone to play in the park. That's when I heard a still, small voice whispering in my ear, one I had heard many times back in Egypt. I don't know how it managed to follow me all the way from Cairo; but there it was in my kitchen as I was sipping my morning tea.

Nathan? What are you doing here in Vancouver? Is this really your life and your people? And what about the ministry I called you to? Have you forgotten about that? I tried to ignore the voice, but it wouldn't go away. After a while I heard a few more sentences. *No, Nathan, this is not your home, and these are not your people. We've had this conversation before. What will your answer be this time?* Then the voice disappeared, leaving me to ponder that final question.

When Susan came home, she could tell something was bothering me. When she asked what it was, I said I was a little homesick but it was nothing. I wasn't about to mention some mysterious voice in my head, and I sure wasn't ready to admit our move may have been a mistake.

Over the next several days there were more of these troubling verbal visits. I even started calling my strange visitor "The Voice." It was much better than admitting it was God's voice I was hearing. It's also easier to turn off a non-person's words than those coming from Someone who lives in your heart. I had learned many years before that if you try to push him to a back shelf, you are only asking for trouble.

Finally, one day I knew it was time to stop these one-way conversations and face up to my dilemma. I certainly didn't want to get into a Good Nathan, Bad Nathan situation again. So when Susan came home, I told her the whole story. And when I finished, she said she had been bothered by these same thoughts.

For the next couple of weeks we wrestled with whether it was God's will for us to go back to Egypt. As we did, I discovered Susan was actually quite homesick. She longed to see her mama, her brother Nabil, her sisters, and a whole list of friends. But no matter how long we talked, we always ended up back at the same question: What about Maggie and Martin?

One morning, as we were sitting in the kitchen sipping tea, we ran out of things to say. I remember looking over at Susan and thinking, *There is really only one option. We need to go back to Cairo, and we must do it now. The longer we wait, the harder it will be on the children.* When I shared my thinking with Susan, she said she had reached the same conclusion several days earlier but hadn't wanted to tell me.

In my usual style, once the decision was made I acted on it quickly. So I headed out to buy the return tickets, even though Susan and I still had some mixed feelings about our situation. But one thing was clear in our minds: God was guiding our thinking, and that made it easier to move ahead.

When we announced to our friends and family that we were moving back to Egypt, it caused a big uproar. The first person I told was my sister Hoda, and at first she thought I was joking. When she realized I was serious, she reacted pretty much as I expected she would.

"Are you crazy, Nathan? You can't do this. Look what you will be giving up. Susan will soon be a licensed pharmacist here, and you will also find your place. And what about

Maggie and Martin? If only for their sake you must stay so they can have a chance for a better life."

It sounded as if she had been preparing her speech for days. When I finally had a chance to get in a few words, I answered with all the patience I could find. "No, Sister, we cannot stay. Susan and I agree that the Lord wants us back in Egypt, and that settles the question. Besides, once God takes control of your life, he helps you see what he is giving you, not what you are giving up."

Our very animated debate went on for several days, until at last my sister could see our decision was final. From then until we left for Cairo, the topic was not discussed again.

For the next several days our family went into what you might call a holding pattern. We tried to explain the move to Maggie and Martin, but they were heartbroken. At just four and six years old, it was impossible for them to grasp what following the leading of the Lord actually meant. They loved their new home, and no matter what we said they didn't want to leave.

At last we came to the day before our departure, and to fill those final hours I walked down the street to a Christian bookstore. While I was browsing through a magazine on the literature table, I noticed an advertisement about Christian teaching materials. My curiosity got the best of me and I decided to dial the phone number to see if these lessons might be useful back in Egypt. Someone answered on the second ring.

"Hello, this is Mel. How may I help you?" His voice sounded warm and friendly.

I briefly explained who I was and a bit about our ministry in Egypt. Then I asked if it was possible for me to get a copy of his materials before we went back home. When Mel discovered I was very close to his office, he immediately asked to take me to lunch. Since everything was packed and ready for our trip, I agreed.

As we ate, I told him about the burden God had given me for my people back home. Mel then said he would like me to meet his board of directors the next morning. I protested that we were scheduled to fly to Cairo that same evening, but when he promised to have me back home by two o'clock, I agreed. After he dropped me back at our flat, however, I thought, *This is crazy. Susan is going to kill me.*

Sure enough, my sweet wife was not happy with my plans. But when Mel picked me up the next day, I wondered if this might turn out to be a divine appointment. He explained that the main purpose of their organization was to partner with national believers who minister to their own people. I thought, *Wow, that's exactly what I do back in Egypt.*

After driving for about an hour, we came to the place where Mel's board was meeting. When we walked inside, there were about ten men gathered around a table eating lunch. Most of their names I have forgotten, but I have come to know two of the men quite well, one of whom was Pastor Don, the board chairman. Once everyone was seated again, Mel gave a brief summary of my ministry, then asked me to tell the board more of my story.

When I finished, we had time for a few questions from several of the men. Then Mel said we needed to be excused, since he had promised to have me back home by two o'clock. One thing I learned about Mel that day: when he tells you he will do something, he keeps his word. So Pastor Don had the men gather around, and he led them in a stirring prayer—for me, my family, and for the people of Egypt. And I'll tell you, Brother Don is one pastor who knows how to pray! It reminded me of the stories they still tell about my grandfather, the Man of Prayer, back in the village of El Sahel.

The next thing I knew we were speeding down the highway on our way back to Susan. As the wheels of the car hummed on the pavement, my head was also spinning. I could hardly believe all that had happened since the previous day. When Mel pulled up to my house we shook hands, said a quick goodbye, and promised to stay in touch. In the coming months Mel did stay in touch, and over the next fifteen years he was the Barnabas-the-Encourager of my life. I learned to know and love this dear man in a very special way.

As I hurried up the sidewalk to our door, the unbelievable events of the past twenty-four hours kept cycling through my mind. I wanted to rush in and share with Susan everything that had happened, but I knew I would have to wait until things settled a bit. Perhaps we could talk on the plane after the children were asleep. Meanwhile, one thought slowly emerged from the fog of my confusion: *Maybe this was why we had to come all the way to Canada. Maybe God had wanted me to meet my new friend Mel.*

13

HOME AGAIN

I walked through the door at exactly two o'clock, but Susan was not all that impressed. She was nervously pacing the floor, afraid we would miss our flight. Maggie and Martin were crying because they still didn't want to go, and just when I got them settled down, there was a knock on the door. Our neighbors who had given us the red couch had come to reclaim it.

Maggie and Martin loved that leather couch. So when the neighbors came to take it away, the children jumped into their usual seats at each end and began to sob. It was their way of telling us they didn't want to leave. But it was too late to think of changing our minds. Our course was set; we were moving back to Cairo.

My sister Hoda and her husband drove us to the airport, we checked in for our flight, and soon it was time to say goodbye. The scene was a complete reversal from our arrival. Instead of a happy celebration, there were long, sad faces and lots of tears. Our relatives still couldn't believe we were leaving. Although they were Christians, it was hard for them to view this as God's will. Many years would pass before they understood it truly was his plan for us.

Our long flight was filled with mixed emotions. The children still didn't understand, no matter how we tried to explain. Our heads wanted to agree with them, but our hearts knew we were doing the right thing. As our plane began its final approach, Susan and I wondered what life would be like for us now. We had been away only three months, but it seemed like an eternity.

We taxied up to the terminal and slowly began pushing our way through passport control. Outside we were surprised to find a sizeable crowd waiting to greet us. We had expected our family to be there, but we didn't expect to see so many faculty and staff from the school. They were accompanied by a large group of students, all of them waving and calling our names.

By God's grace our small flat was still empty and we moved right back in. It gave us a comfortable feeling, like an old pair of shoes. Before we finished unpacking that day, Mama walked in the door carrying Baba's walking staff. It seemed like the Lord was saying, *Look, Nathan; this is where you belong.*

Almost from the day we arrived, a steady stream of people began coming to seek advice from both Susan and me. In addition to the natural bonds with our students, we also had built close relationships with their parents. They often came to us for guidance in more than school subjects, asking to hear about basic spiritual and moral principles too. As one parent had said earlier, they wanted us to "teach them how to raise their children to a good life."

Among those who were the most happy for our return were brothers Ruven and Benjamin, two Messianic believers I had met at their home in Jerusalem some years earlier. Shortly after our arrival back in Cairo they came to visit us for a few days, and as on previous trips they stayed in our home. Since we had no guest room they slept in our bedroom, while we happily made ourselves comfortable on the living room floor.

As the brothers were about to go back to Jerusalem, Ruven said they had a gift for us. He pulled a bulging envelope from his pocket and handed it to me. When I looked inside, I saw a large sum of money—five thousand dollars! For once in my life, I was totally speechless. I finally managed to stammer, "What . . . what is this?"

Ruven was smiling broadly as he replied, "The next time we come we will sleep in your new house. This is for the down payment." I don't know why we were surprised. We should have known that when God blessed Susan and me with children, he would provide a suitable place for us to live.

We picked up at the school right where we had left off before moving to Vancouver. Our fine staff now numbered forty, and they were more than happy to go back to the way things had been organized prior to our sudden exodus. With a steadily growing enrollment over the prior six years, we had reached our maximum capacity of 350 students, and over 60 percent were from Muslim families. Several seemed to come from the more extreme Islamic branches, judging from their fathers' long beards and dark robes. Apparently even these parents were attracted to the high moral and educational standards we maintained.

One day while walking in the neighborhood I passed an orphanage for very poor girls located near our school. They had been rescued from some of the most terrible living conditions you can imagine. The orphanage was able to provide only their basic daily needs, which did not include education. As a result, they had no real hope of achieving a better life.

My heart ached whenever I passed by this place. It reminded me that Baba had grown up in a children's home, and that I had also been a fatherless boy. But our situations had been different in one very significant way: we had both been able to attend school.

I decided that we needed to help these girls by providing free enrollment at our school and other practical helps such as school uniforms, books, and other necessities. We even arranged counseling for those who needed to deal with more serious issues. It was a joy to see them blossom into bright young ladies. Many have gone on to earn university degrees and are now happy wives and mothers.

In spite of these blessings, our return to Cairo was not one big bed of roses. All of the problems we had tried to escape by running to Canada were still there. In fact, many of them had become worse. But one thing had changed, and for the better: our hearts. The Lord gave us a Bible verse, 1 John 4:18, that says "love casts out fear," and we found it to be true. We were so filled with love for the people around us that we didn't have much room for fear. Still, there were often situations in which we called for God's guardian angels to protect us.

As classes were about to begin one term, we needed to add a teacher. Several good applicants were interviewed and one seemed to be a perfect match. We knew she was a Muslim, but she appeared to have a kind heart and good teaching skills. Furthermore, we were required by law to have a Muslim teach our Arabic classes, so we hired her.

Shortly after school began, one of our Christian students came to me in tears. "Sir, my Arabic teacher says no one goes to heaven except by worshiping Mohammed. When I told her my Sunday school teacher says we must accept Jesus, she slapped me, then told me to leave class and not come back. What should I do?"

I told her not to worry, I would take care of things. When we conducted a quiet investigation, we found the teacher had gone to the authorities with accusations that I was a radical Christian who hated all Muslim students and persecuted them—in short, that I made their lives miserable. This is a very serious charge against a school and its leader, and it can lead to huge fines, closing of the school, or even imprisonment.

The authorities immediately launched their own inquiry to determine if the charges were true. They personally interviewed other Muslim staff members and several Muslim parents. All of their sessions were held in private and I had no opportunity to answer the charges in any way.

Throughout the investigation, every single person testified that the teacher's accusations were completely false. They described me as a fair and impartial man who treated everyone in a kind, loving way. So rather than punishing me, the authorities convicted the teacher of bringing false charges and she was dismissed from the school. God's angels had taken care of us once again.

This is only one example of what we dealt with day in and day out. Not long after our return, those late-night phone calls started up again. As before, I would be ordered to appear for impromptu interviews. Susan would become quite frightened, wondering when—even if—I would return. She would pray nonstop until I finally walked back into our flat. After a while, I came to expect the phone to ring, but I never fully escaped the anxious feelings those calls produced.

In spite of such problems, we soon had all of our programs running smoothly again. God blessed us with a team of top-notch workers, and this soon enabled me to take on another new challenge. The area of children's ministry continued to be a primary focus for me, and over time I became concerned about the quality of teaching in most children's ministries.

Whenever I was invited to speak to local congregations, I would often sit in on the children's meetings. It was easy to see that the high standards we employed in our day school were not present in many children's ministries. Most leaders were simply telling familiar Bible stories about Moses, Esther, David and Goliath, and others. They were not teaching basic Bible doctrine or the central elements of our Christian faith.

When I mentioned this to pastors and church leaders, many of them said they shared my concerns. Several asked me to develop a curriculum to teach these important truths in children's terms. It seems I had just stumbled across a basic principle: don't point out a problem unless you are ready to provide a solution. Soon I found myself submerged in an enormous writing project.

After two years of hard work, intense research, writing, and rewriting, I completed *Creative Bible Lessons for Children*. The series consisted of sixteen books, each with twenty-six lessons. This meant that two books would provide lessons for one full year. And one feature made it unique: it was in the Arabic language. It was the first time such a resource had been published anywhere in the Arab world.

There was a second important feature to the series. Each book included one chapter on the birth and life of Christ. At the end of that chapter is a specific opportunity for each child to accept Jesus as their personal Savior. This was the central purpose of the whole curriculum.

All the time I was writing the lessons, there was one critical requirement that had to be kept in mind: in order to publish any religious teaching materials in Egypt, they must be approved by the Ministry of Education. So when the series was completed, I submitted it to the authorities. Gaining their approval was by no means assured.

The government officials who review such materials follow specific guidelines. Their three main concerns are (1) that the lessons contain no political statements of any kind, (2) that they be used only in churches (meaning evangelical churches), and (3) that they contain no material, either positive or negative, about any specific religious group or denomination. These criteria must be followed for publications from any group that might be considered "questionable." But after waiting nervously for several months, we were finally given permission to print and distribute the curriculum. However, we knew this approval could be withdrawn at any time and for any reason—or no reason at all. But that uncertainty would need to be left in God's hands.

The next step in helping churches make use of our lessons was to conduct teacher training classes throughout the country. By the time we finished, over five thousand teachers were ready to launch the program. The series found broad approval across denominational lines as well, with more than 450 churches in Egypt alone using the materials. Word soon spread to several other Arabic-speaking nations, and they began requesting copies.

God miraculously overcame many obstacles with this project. One such instance involved the district leader of a large traditional denomination. When this priest heard about our lessons, he contacted me and requested copies. After looking them over he said he would like to adopt the series for all of the churches in his region. He also invited me to train teachers throughout his district to use the material. We agreed on a training strategy and set dates for me to begin. And that's when we suddenly encountered a serious roadblock.

Before we could get our training seminars underway, someone reported this godly leader to the national office of his denomination. A formal inquiry was undertaken and he was called to face charges before a council of inquiry. He phoned me to explain the whole matter. His closing words were, "This Sunday I will conduct my service in the morning, then appear before the council in the afternoon. It could possibly be my last sermon." I promised my entire children's ministry committee would hold him up in prayer.

The council was set for one o'clock in the afternoon and we began praying at that very hour, agreeing not to stop until we received a call from the priest. We were convinced that without a miraculous intervention by the Lord, the situation would not turn out well.

Later that afternoon my phone rang. As soon as I answered, the priest blurted out, "A vote was taken and your materials have been unanimously approved!" My children's committee burst into praises to God when I told them. After things quieted down, he explained what had taken place.

"The meeting began with many angry charges against me. Strong feelings were voiced that I should be disciplined, possibly even expelled from the ministry. But one influential leader knows you, Nathan, and he began to carefully read your materials during the meeting. After a few minutes, he asked to speak.

"'My friends,' he said, 'these are very serious charges against our fellow clergyman. I have been reading through the lessons this afternoon, and I see they contain very good Bible teaching. They are solid in content, attractive in appearance, and clearly at a good level for children. Here, let me show you.' He then pointed out several key passages.

"I couldn't believe what happened next. After the council looked more carefully at your lessons, the atmosphere in the room completely changed. The man then said to the group, 'Gentlemen, I recommend we adopt this curriculum for all the churches in our district and that we invite Nathan to hold training seminars for our teachers.' They added only one requirement. Your name must not appear on the book covers.

"When the chairman of the council called for a vote on the recommendation, it was approved unanimously. A second resolution was also passed making it clear that I would not be reprimanded in any way for my part in this matter."

Because of the courage of one godly priest, we have now trained some six hundred teachers in his district. They are using our curriculum with more than twenty thousand children throughout the entire region. Only God can tell how many young lives will be eternally changed as a result.

———

With our curriculum project now completed, I was able to turn my attention to what I refer to as a world missions mentality. Due to the long-standing problems Egyptian believers have faced inside our country, the Christian community has generally focused on our own spiritual situation. There was little understanding of the term "global Christian," and there was almost no vision for proclaiming the gospel beyond our borders.

As my international travels increased, I became more aware of the passage in Matthew 28, commonly called the Great Commission. I felt the Lord was saying that "go into all the world and preach the gospel" was a message for believers in my country. So I began preaching on this theme, then taking small evangelistic teams to Jordan, Syria, Sudan, and other Arabic-speaking countries. We immediately saw a remarkable response to this teaching in our churches, and now several of them are catching the vision of spreading the gospel outside our borders.

I've often thanked the Lord for bringing us back home to Egypt, and for blessing our many programs. Those were good days for us, both as a family and in ministry. But there came a day when I had to admit our workload had reached its absolute limits. So I decided under no circumstances would we consider launching any new programs or participating in any new conferences. It was time to concentrate on what we were already doing.

Then, just when I was feeling good about this wise decision, I received an unusual invitation.

14

GOOD FRIDAY

2000–2003
CAIRO TO KOREA

In the year 2000 the world said goodbye to the twentieth century and hello to the twenty-first. In spite of all the wild predictions of disaster and end times in the new millennium, the desert sun continued to rise each morning in Cairo and few things changed. The same can be said about life for Susan and me.

Words cannot express the joy our two children brought to the family. Maggie's bubbly personality kept all of us energized. Each passing year she became more helpful to her mother and me, and soon her natural leadership qualities began to blossom. She excelled in school and was involved in children's activities at church.

Martin was no less of a blessing. One of his greatest traits was his obedient nature. Even when he occasionally mis-behaved he would quickly admit his mistake, which made him easy to forgive. He also earned top marks at school, but he was more quiet and easygoing than his sister, for which we were thankful. I'm not sure we could have kept up with two high-energy kids like Maggie.

Just before Christmas, Susan and I welcomed one more special-delivery package from the Lord. We often call our son Michael our "millennial blessing," and the fact that he was a surprise made him even more special. It was truly a thrill for me to be a new father again. Watching our son grow from a tiny infant to a boy, and now into a teenager, has added a unique dimension to our lives.

During those growing-up years in the family, our ministry also continued to mature. In many ways it was a relief to be in a no-new-ministries mode. It enabled me to refine the numerous programs we were already operating. It also gave me time to reflect on ways the Lord had blessed us in the past and where he might be leading us in the future.

Over the next couple of years, without my noticing, a small tug-of-war was building inside me. I continued to preach about becoming global Christians while also proclaiming that our ministry would make no new commitments. Looking back, this conflict of ideas seems obvious, but at the time I didn't see it. Once again, God sent an unexpected message to wake me up.

One bright September day in 2003, I was studying in my office when the phone rang. On the other end was Brother Kim, who pastored a Korean congregation in Cairo. We had met through a fellowship of Christian workers in Cairo and become quite good friends. He would often visit me at home or at the office to seek my advice, and I had spoken in his church on several occasions.

After a few brief words of greeting, Pastor Kim got right to the point. The South Korean ambassador had called from the embassy, asking if my friend knew someone from Egypt who could speak at a highly regarded international conference in Seoul. It was being organized by the South Korean government, under the sponsorship of the former prime minister. An impressive list of prominent people from around the world would be participating, and they wanted someone from Egypt to represent the Middle East. The theme of the conference was centered on nonviolence movements around the world.

Brother Kim immediately thought of me, and told the ambassador, "Sir, I have a friend who would be perfect." With no hesitation, the ambassador authorized the pastor to invite me and, if I accepted, to make all the necessary arrangements on his behalf.

This invitation was a complete surprise, and for a moment I didn't know how to respond. It sounded like lots of other conferences where I had spoken, but the fact that it was being held in Korea caught my attention. One of my dreams had been to visit what was known then as the world's largest church, located in the city of Seoul. Thinking this might be my only opportunity, I agreed to go. My no-new-commitments pledge didn't even enter my mind. Only after my arrival would I discover this was not a Christian conference. Somehow I had missed that tiny detail.

Preparing for the conference was relatively easy, since I simply planned to speak about my ministry. However, as the date drew near, emails from the conference director began to arrive, asking for the title of my address, a detailed outline, and any charts or other materials that would be used in my presentation. I promised to send them, but never got around to it.

On the appointed November day, I boarded a plane to Korea and settled back in my seat for the long flight. Everything was just fine—until I landed in Seoul. That's when I got my first big shock. Since the conference was being sponsored by the South Korean government, a personal escort was waiting to accompany me everywhere. He led me out to a sleek private limousine, which chauffeured me to an extremely expensive five-star hotel. I thought, *Nathan, you have really done it this time*.

My escort made sure everything in the room was satisfactory, then said, "Doctor, you must be tired from your travel. Why don't you rest for a while? This evening we will drive you to the opening ceremonies and reception." With a formal bow, he then turned and left.

When we arrived that evening, my second surprise was waiting. All of the guest speakers, including me, were introduced to the Korean prime minister and countless other national and international dignitaries. We were given fancy name badges identifying us as "Dr. This" or "Dr. That," followed by the country from which we came and our professions. Mine simply said "Dr. Nathan . . . Egypt . . . Journalist." I thought, *What's going on here? I'm not a journalist.*

During the reception I learned more about the other sixteen guests. They came from all around the world. One was the president of Shanghai University and another was a Nobel Prize winner from India. I met a scholar from Russia and a representative of a famous university in America—Harvard, I believe—and the rest were just as impressive. Doctor Nelson Mandela had been invited, but he was too ill to travel. Instead, the Korean ambassador to South Africa would deliver his address.

At that moment I felt extremely insignificant. Here I was, just plain "Nathan, from Egypt," rubbing shoulders with some of the most distinguished scholars in the world. Even the title on my name badge was incorrect. Then when it seemed things could not get any worse, they did. As the evening came to a close, the conference director marched up to me and delivered a third and final jolt.

"Dr. Nathan, every guest speaker has provided an outline to their address except you. I must have yours, first thing tomorrow morning." He had a few more stern words for me, along with several probing questions. When he discovered I was a Christian leader in Egypt, he got right to the point.

"Perhaps you misunderstand, Doctor. This is not a Christian conference. You were not invited here to preach. You are to limit your remarks to the topic of nonviolence and what you believe to be the solution to the ongoing conflicts in the Middle East. Please keep that in mind."

He abruptly ended our conversation and rushed off to take care of other matters. My mind was in turmoil on the way back to the hotel. What could I say about the hostilities between Arabs, Jews, and Christians in our part of the world? These bitter clashes have been going on for centuries. How was I supposed to come up with a solution on such short notice?

My stomach was in knots when we drove up to the hotel. I definitely had to come up with something to give the conference director, but my thoughts were a confused mess. I finally sat down and wrote a simple one-page outline stating some of the same tired, overworked theories about the conflicts between Middle Eastern people groups. It ended with a few lame-sounding ideas for bringing these people together to resolve their longstanding differences. Then, feeling like a total failure, I fell into bed.

The main conference sessions were being held in the Houses of Parliament, and when I walked in the next morning the director was waiting. Without a word, I handed him my brief outline. He glanced at it quickly, then looked at me with a frown.

"Is this all you have? No PowerPoint presentation? No charts or handouts? Surely you have something more."

"No, that is all."

He looked again at my outline, then back at me. Without another word, he shook his head and slowly walked away. He was probably thinking, *What a disaster. Dr. Nathan will be the worst speaker of the entire conference.* At that moment I would have readily agreed.

When we were shown our places on the platform, my seat was beside the Nobel Prize winner from India. He would speak first and I would follow. This tall, stately gentleman was dressed in his colorful native robe, while the rest of us wore suits and ties. The stark contrast in our apparel made me feel even worse. I wanted to disappear.

Our conference guidelines allotted each speaker one hour for his address. The Indian scholar stepped to the lectern and announced the topic of his address: "Consider Mahatma Gandhi: His Life and Teachings." These writings, he solemnly declared, contained the principles that would end all the violence in our world. It was a most impressive and convincing presentation.

The longer he spoke, the more nervous I became. My mind recalled my Bible study blunder, when a certain teenager thought he was so wise. On this occasion it seemed clear I did not have all the answers, so this time I wanted the earth to swallow me *before* my address, not after.

When the man from India sat down, they announced

my name. As I walked slowly to the podium my knees were shaking. Seated before me were the prime minister and three hundred distinguished guests. In a booth upstairs were translators in headphones, waiting to relay my speech to those who did not speak English. Several TV cameras were aimed at me, poised to capture my every word. The cameras looked like guns, and I almost wished they would shoot me.

At that moment I whispered a short, desperate prayer: "Jesus, help me. Let my words glorify you, just as the last man tried to glorify Gandhi."

After my prayer the Lord filled my heart with peace, and I knew whatever came out would honor him. So I forgot about my notes, cleared my throat, and began to speak.

"Ladies and gentlemen, first let me apologize. I have no handouts, no PowerPoint, no charts. All I have is my Bible, so let me begin today by sharing my personal story." Then I described the heart-wrenching events of Black Friday, ending with the birth of my hate-filled passion for revenge. It was not my intention to shock them. I simply wanted to paint a picture of what violence really looked like in my part of the world as seen through six-year-old eyes.

I paused briefly and looked around the room. It seemed everyone was frozen in place, with their eyes glued to me. After a deep breath, I continued. "It is important for you to understand one thing: I'm not proud of my lust for revenge. But these feelings are a natural reaction to violence anywhere in the world, and that includes the Middle East. The normal response to violence is always more violence. Let me say that again: violence creates more violence.

"You may ask what makes me so sure. It is because, for five long years, I lived with a heart filled with hatred for those terrorists. And if I had continued in that condition, you would surely be looking at a murderer standing before you this morning. But then something changed. Really, I should say Someone changed me.

"One night, I met a Person—a real, living Person—and he totally changed my life. This Person's name is Jesus, and in my Bible it says he is the Prince of Peace. He took away my hatred and passion for revenge and replaced them with a spirit of peace." I paused again, afraid the people were not accepting my words. But from the looks on their faces it was clear they were all listening.

"Let me tell you another story, also from the Middle East." I opened my Bible to chapter 26 of Matthew's gospel, which records the arrest of Jesus before his crucifixion. I pointed out how one of his friends responded with violence by pulling out a sword and slashing off the ear of the high priest's servant. But Jesus told Peter to put away his sword, then healed the man's ear.

The rest of my allotted hour was spent talking about Jesus, explaining that he was the only true solution for violence. I told them my life was evidence that he can completely remove hatred and replace it with love for those who attack us. I ended by restating my main theme: Jesus was the only true solution for violence.

There was not a sound in the room as I turned and walked from the podium. I thought, *No one will understand . . . no one will accept my words*. But before I reached my seat a wave of applause swept across the hall. When I turned, the entire audience was standing as they continued to applaud. I didn't know what to do, so I simply whispered, "Dear Lord, thank you. This applause is for you."

After the morning session, the prime minister rushed forward and embraced me. "Doctor Nathan, thank you for those moving words. I am also a Christian. Your address this morning was powerful and honoring to God." Several others came to offer similar warm remarks.

When our meeting reconvened I took my assigned seat beside the scholar from India. In my heart there was an indescribable peace. God had given me the right words that day, and again I whispered, "Jesus, thank you for answering my prayer."

Before our session began the next morning, the Indian gentleman asked to speak privately with me. He seemed troubled, and I will never forget his words.

"Thank you, sir, for your profound words about Jesus yesterday," he said. "I have never heard this before and my heart was deeply moved. I must know more, but our time today is filled with lectures. Would you be kind enough to meet me tomorrow for breakfast?" He suggested an early time so we would not be rushed.

The following morning he was waiting in the restaurant. As we ate breakfast he asked many probing questions—about me, my life, and about Jesus. He listened with great respect to all I had to say. We talked long after our food was gone, and by the time we parted the tender seeds of salvation had been planted in this dear old gentleman. Then it was up to the Lord to make the seeds grow. In my heart I firmly believe that the truth of God's Word delivered through me enabled him to make his eternal decision.

The closing session of the conference convened on Friday morning. There was another very dignified ceremony during which several awards and recognitions were announced. My flight home was scheduled to depart shortly after we adjourned, so I sat in the back row dressed in a plain T-shirt and casual trousers. As usual I was daydreaming, when I heard the conference leader say, "Now it is time to present our final and most important award: the Peace Prize.

"As you know, our organization was founded by American president Ronald Reagan. I'm sure he would be greatly honored by the fine lectures delivered this week by this distinguished group of scholars. As our meetings come to a close, we want to honor the man who clearly delivered the most outstanding address of the entire conference. We will present to him this morning our most prestigious Peace Prize." After a short, rather dramatic pause, he looked in my direction and said, "His name is Dr. Nathan."

Suddenly I felt weak all over. Loud applause broke out as people rose to their feet and turned my way. When ushers came to escort me to the platform, I could hardly get out of my seat. At the front of the hall, a long black robe was placed around me. (That took care of my casual attire.) The official proclamation was formally read and a medallion and certificate were presented to me, followed by another hearty round of applause. Then the director declared the conference closed.

Several people came to offer personal congratulation as the audience exited the hall. I said a quick and courteous goodbye to the conference officials, then rushed to the car that was waiting to drive me to the airport. My trusty escort guided me through the VIP line and onto the plane just as the door was closing.

As we pushed back from the gate, I started thinking through all that had happened over the past week. Something inside told me that God had arranged this trip for my benefit. The overwhelming response to my presentation had made an impact not only on the other conferees but also on me. Somewhere on that long flight home, I realized as never before that the love of Jesus truly *is* the answer, not simply for violence, but for all the evil in our world. The significance of that truth would become even more evident in the years ahead.

By the time my plane touched down in Cairo, another thought began to blossom in my mind like a beautiful rose.

In the past when I had shared my story about Black Friday, it always left me with a bad feeling about all Fridays. But after my week in Korea I knew that would no longer be true, since the day the conference ended had turned out to be a very good Friday for me.

My thoughts then took me back to another Friday almost two thousand years ago . . . the day our Lord Jesus was crucified. Today we refer to that day as Good Friday, but it didn't seem good at the time. And I began to smile as I realized that now Black Friday could stay in my past, and I could look forward to many more good Fridays in my future.

15

BURNING CHURCHES, LOVING HEARTS

ARAB SPRING AND BEYOND
EGYPT AND THE MIDDLE EAST

Late in 2010 a movement of unrest and turmoil erupted in the Middle East, beginning in Tunisia and spreading throughout much of the Arab world. Tensions and frustrations leading up to these events did not appear overnight. They had been bubbling beneath the surface for many years. Spontaneous street demonstrations led to more volatile confrontations, and in many cases these escalated to full-blown uprisings against national governments.

Soon world news outlets were reporting these violent and deadly scenes. Some journalists referred to these events as the

"Arab Spring," but it was nothing at all like spring. Radical groups quickly rose up to take advantage of the instability, intent on seizing control of national governments and imposing their will on the people all across the region. Instead of the sunrise of a bright new day, we saw a dark cloud of oppression descend on countries from Tunisia to Syria.

While reasons for the uprisings varied from one country to the next, there were several common factors that partially explained these horrific events. One major cause was a general collapse of economic conditions throughout the region. Prices of everyday necessities such as food, housing, and utilities shot up, and the disease of unemployment became an epidemic. Those who had jobs saw their salaries plummet, and the value of our currencies dropped at an alarming rate.

A second cause of the unrest can be traced to what I will refer to as empty promises. Our leaders claimed to be in favor of free democracy, but people knew it wasn't true. What we were told and what we observed just didn't match up. All around us we could see a small, privileged minority selfishly hoarding more and more for themselves while everyone else gradually became increasingly poor.

Finally the have-nots decided they had suffered long enough. Things had to change—and now, not later. They began banding together to demand better lives for themselves and their children. As demonstrations continued to spread across the region, young people were a large, vocal, and oftentimes violent part of these encounters.

In late December this hideous monster of violence raised its ugly head in Egypt, and everything began to unravel. As conditions continued to deteriorate, certain radical elements took this opportunity to confront Christians in many parts of the country. Many of these confrontations led to physical assaults, and some even resulted in killings. One of the most shocking attacks occurred on December 31 at a church in Alexandria.

About one thousand believers had gathered that evening for their traditional New Year's Eve service. During prayer time they felt a strong sense that Christians were going to be faced with something big in 2011. So they began calling out to God for protection in the coming year.

The clock had just passed midnight and the service was about to end when a massive car bomb exploded outside. Panicked people both inside and out stampeded in all directions. Agonized screams for help filled the air. A seventeen-year-old victim reported from his hospital bed, "The last thing I heard was a powerful explosion, and then my ears went deaf. I could see body parts scattered all over."

What had been a place of prayer now looked like a war zone. More than thirty people were killed and over one hundred injured in that grisly attack.

However, what the terrorists intended to be a devastating blow to believers actually drew them together. It was clear that Christians were being targeted by the radicals, and believers decided they had suffered enough. An attack of this magnitude demanded a response—but rather than continuing the cycle of violence, they decided to band together in prayer.

Throughout Egypt believers from all denominations began organizing all-night prayer vigils. Some became too large to meet in churches, so they started gathering in large parks, arenas, and other public places. One prayer service grew to over forty thousand believers, all calling on God to control and guide the events in our country.

Most of what followed over the next several weeks and months has been widely reported by journalists and TV outlets around the world. So I will highlight only a few key events and explain how they impacted our ministry in Egypt. On January 25, millions of people—many of them young adults—poured into the streets and public squares of towns and cities all across the country, shouting and chanting for freedom, justice, and a better life.

The turmoil and unrest continued for eighteen chaotic days. Demands for government leaders to step down grew louder with each passing hour. When these leaders were finally forced to resign in early February, you could almost hear people take a deep breath in anticipation of a better life. But soon it became obvious these dreams would not be realized. Instead, a fanatic minority group known as the Muslim Brotherhood manipulated political events and seized control of the country—first the parliament, then other government offices, and finally the presidency. We quickly found that rather than the pressure easing, it would actually increase.

Once again we found ourselves locked in a downward spiral. Economic conditions became more desperate as many factories were shut down and hundreds of prominent business leaders began to abandon their homeland. The group that suffered most was the Christian community. In the period of only one month more than forty Egyptian churches were set ablaze. But again, rather than meeting violence with violence, Christians answered these attacks with a simple statement: "You burned our churches, but we still love you." This soon became the motto of believers throughout Egypt.

As these deplorable attacks continued, most news outlets either ignored those with a Christian connection or concentrated on events in Cairo and other urban centers. Sadly, some of the greatest atrocities were imposed on believers in rural villages. Many were forced to run for their lives, leaving homes and possessions behind. These possessions were then handed over to people who matched the desired political beliefs of the radical terrorists.

This reign of terror forced numerous churches to close their doors. Many that had not been trashed or burned stopped holding services simply because their members had been forced to flee. Naturally, with no services there were no offerings, which meant no income for pastors. One Islamic leader publicly declared, "If it is so bad for Christians here, let them get out of Egypt." Many took his advice and left, looking for a new home in any country where they could live in peace.

Our family was no different. As these pressures and dangers pressed in upon us, our relatives kept calling and begging us to leave. My sister Hoda had relocated from Vancouver to California, where my brother Magdy now lived, and my brother Onsey had settled in London after university. All three continuously rang us with one urgent plea: hurry up and get out, before it's too late!

Again we faced the vexing question of whether to leave or stay, but this time our children made the decision more complex. Maggie had finished her university degree, Martin was still in college, and Michael was about to start secondary school. We talked openly with them about our situation and what the options were. We already had visas permitting us to move to the United States, so that was a possibility. But just as we had when facing this decision before, the last Person we talked to was the Lord.

It wasn't long before we heard God's clear reply: our place was with our people in Egypt, encouraging and lifting them up in their time of trouble. But this time we heard God telling us to minister not only to believers but also to reach out to nonbelievers.

Everywhere we looked, there were hurting people. No longer would it be enough to simply minister to their spiritual issues; they also had urgent practical needs that demanded attention. There were shopkeepers whose shops had been torched, others with desperate medical conditions, and many with no jobs and no way to feed their loved ones. How could we talk about Jesus, the Bread of Life, when people had no bread on the table?

It was obvious a new strategy was required to address these challenges, so we gathered our ministry team and discussed ways to respond. We agreed from the start that our message would never change, but our methods would. Let me express it in these words: we began to reach out with the Bible in one hand and bread in the other. As we did, smiles began to reappear on people's faces and hope started shining in their eyes.

One way we implemented our new strategy was by opening a medical center in a town of about five thousand that didn't even have a local doctor. With the help of some Christian businessmen, we established a clinic to serve the whole district. News of the clinic spread quickly, and soon more than ten doctors had volunteered to work there and treat patients free of charge.

A second practical help we provided was blankets for poor families. While our winters are not as severe as those in North America, the nights are still quite cool and many families were forced to sleep on the bare floor, with neither bed nor bedding. We began distributing hundreds of blankets each year to help ease this problem.

School-age children also felt the impact of those dark days. So we distributed school uniforms and classroom materials to more than one thousand students. Our terrible economic conditions had made it impossible for poor parents to provide these items, and without them their children would not be admitted to classes.

These programs and others like them opened doors of outreach to our Muslim neighbors. When they asked why we would help them after the way the Christians had been treated, we simply replied, "Because we love you and Jesus loves you. He died for the whole world, including you." As a result, many were receptive to the message of Jesus Christ.

As we tried to improve the physical and spiritual conditions of those around us, life continued to get worse under the new regime. To say the results of our first revolution in 2011 were a disappointment is an understatement. For the vast majority of Egyptians conditions became increasingly unbearable with each passing day.

Hardly a day went by without some radical new regulation being imposed. No area of society was overlooked. The school curriculum was revised, women were treated almost as non-humans, and our ancient artwork and historic sites were suddenly taboo. The new government wanted to control everything and everybody.

One day these pressures stopped being political and turned personal. As I was driving along a main avenue in Cairo, I was stopped at a police checkpoint. Several armed officers surrounded my car and ordered me out. As one man questioned me the others searched my car, where one officer found Baba's walking staff in the trunk.

"This is a dangerous weapon," he snapped. "We must keep it."

"Take anything of mine you like, but please don't take that." My answer got everyone's attention and I was quickly surrounded by six angry policemen.

"Why shouldn't we take it? What makes this old stick so important?"

"It belonged to my Baba, and it is a symbol of God's goodness to me," I explained. Then I told them about that day in Karya Maghola.

When I finished, the police officer stepped back and looked at his captain. After a few seconds the captain nodded and I was waved back into my car. Only then did the officer pass Baba's staff through the window. Then he took two steps back and simply said, "Go."

The tidal wave of persecution continued throughout the country until one tragic event sparked international outrage. Two terrorists with automatic weapons, knives, and small bombs attacked a wedding ceremony in a Cairo suburb. Many were killed, including an eight-year-old flower girl dressed in her white gown. Her picture was on television screens and in newspapers around the globe. What had begun as a happy marriage ceremony turned out to be a funeral.

In the face of such persecution, believers from all denominations banded together for mutual encouragement and protection. They began calling out to God, saying, "Where are you, Lord? Why don't you answer our cries?" It seemed this long, dark night would never end. The pressure continued to build, until finally on June 30, 2013, things exploded again.

Over thirty million people—nearly one third of our nation's population—poured into the streets from one end of the country to the other. Men and women, boys and girls—people from every age, economic group, and educational background joined the demonstrations. No one wanted to be left out this time. As the crowds chanted and cheered, one central theme was repeated time and again: "We refuse to live under this tyranny. This is our life and our country, and you will not take it from us!"

Unlike in 2011, the army decided to support the Egyptian people in this second revolution. Within three days the entire radical regime, from the president on down, was swept aside. On July 3 a temporary government was installed, new elections were announced, and work was begun on a new constitution. The latest chapter of Egyptian history was being written right before our eyes.

These changes had an immediate and positive impact on believers. After suffering three years of persecution and fear, we could now raise our heads and begin to see hope on the horizon. All of our problems were not solved, but at least we were moving in the right direction. And I could see that, just as I had turned from revenge to redemption, it was now time for all Christians in Egypt to do the same.

All around us non-Christians could see evidence of the way believers had been treated by the Islamic extremists. Our

Muslim neighbors saw the ashes of burned churches. They had witnessed the beatings—even murders—of friends and neighbors, simply because they were followers of Jesus. But they also saw the loving way Christians responded. They could see with their own eyes that we walked the walk, and didn't just talk the talk. When friends and neighbors asked about our response, we continued to say that Jesus loves everyone, no matter who they may be.

Through all of those turbulent days my mind often went back to the address I had delivered in Korea. I recalled crying out for the Lord's help that day, and I clearly remembered the words he gave me: Jesus is the only true solution for violence.

My thoughts sometimes also took me back even further, to the day I accepted Jesus as Savior. I remembered the Lord saying, *Nathan, you must forgive the men who killed your father.* Slowly I began to realize these words were at the absolute center of what God wanted to say to my people.

We needed to lay aside our hatred and passion to get even. It was time to turn from revenge to redemption.

This was the message my people need to hear, not just that day, but every day until Jesus returns to this earth. It is not jihad that can solve the problems we face in these troubled times—it is Jesus. Only by turning to the Prince of Peace can we find true peace, both in our world and, more importantly, in our own lives. This is the message God has burned deep into my heart, and it is the message I must proclaim to my people as long as God gives me strength.

16

BACK TO KARYA MAGHOLA

SEPTEMBER 2013
UPPER EGYPT

The distant crowing of a rooster told me I was back once more in the tiny village of Karya Maghola, except it wasn't so tiny anymore. This day it was more like a small town, but it still seemed like a village to me. The hot desert sun still baked the barren landscape, Pharaoh's chickens still traced lazy circles in the sky, and the narrow winding streets remained wrapped in a blanket of brown dust. As I said before, it is always dusty in Karya Maghola.

I have returned many times to this place that was my home more than fifty years ago—so many times, in fact, that these visits all seem to run together. In the early years they always triggered sad and painful memories. The little village church was still on that same narrow street right next to Ibrahim's shop, and the pastor's home was still upstairs. When I stood and looked out my old bedroom window I was reminded of that night fifty-plus years ago, the night when I shook my fists toward Dark Mountain and vowed to kill the men who had killed my Baba.

Years have passed, and all of that has changed. Why? Not because the village has changed, but because I have been changed—radically and forever changed—by the power of God and the love of his Son. You see, when Jesus moves into your heart and makes it his home, there is no longer any room for hatred or revenge. When Jesus moves in, he wants to occupy your whole heart.

I will always remember this particular trip to Karya Maghola for a very special reason. It was shortly after our second revolution on June 30, 2013. In some ways it was almost as emotional for me as Black Friday. Now that the dark days since 2011 were behind us, the faces of people in the village held a bright message of hope. Not everyone was happy, of course, since many in Upper Egypt still support the radical movement.

On this particular trip I had been asked to bring the Sunday morning message in Baba's last church. I still recall the tender emotions on people's faces that day. It's a memory I will cherish for the rest of my life.

There had been many occasions over the years when I had stood in Baba's pulpit, but this Lord's Day was different in two ways. First, it was a great day of celebration for the believers, and they lifted their voices in thanks to God for bringing them through three long years of terror and trials. When it was time for my sermon, I opened God's Word and shared the message he had given me for that day. The Scripture was from 2 Timothy 1:7, where it says God has given us a spirit of hope, not one of fear.

The day was also very special for me personally for a second reason. As I was speaking that morning, my heart was unusually moved by the thought that I was standing right where Baba had stood to preach. Behind me was the chair where I always sat while listening to him preach, my Bible opened on my lap and my attention riveted to his every word.

Before me that morning were brothers and sisters in Christ, men on one side and ladies on the other, just as they had sat back in Baba's time. The only difference was now they sat on simple benches rather than the bare dirt floor. There were even a few long-time members in the service who had been friends with Baba and Mama. Ibrahim, our dear neighbor who had survived the Black Friday attack, was not there though. He had recently joined Youssef and Baba in heaven with the Lord.

At times like this my mind takes me back to those early days, and I begin to dream again just like I did when I was a boy. But now I don't dream so much about the future; I dream about a past that was never meant to be. I wonder what my life might have looked like if there had been no

Black Friday. I ask myself, *If Baba had lived, where would I be today, and what would I be doing?*

Of course, there is really no way to know that, is there? Maybe I would be living in some small village like Karya Maghola. Perhaps I would be a shopkeeper like Ibrahim, or just a simple farmer, or maybe even a strawberry merchant. Who knows where my path would have taken me?

Instead, I have been privileged to minister for the Lord in so many ways and in so many far-flung places—places I had only read about in books, never thinking in my wildest dreams I might go there some day. I have preached in churches all over the world and been involved in a variety of ministries throughout the Middle East, Africa, Asia, and North America. I have shared my story before world leaders and prime ministers and proclaimed the message of Jesus Christ in more places than I can remember. God has poured blessing upon blessing on my life.

Please don't misunderstand—I'm not telling you these things in a boasting way. I only want to show how the God of the universe can use a simple man, one who was once a little boy in the tiny Egyptian village of Karya Maghola, to bring glory to his name. And I must tell you one more thing, something I hope you will never forget: if the Lord can do this for me, he can do the same for you, if you will trust him to take control of your life.

Whenever I reflect on the events of my life—both the good and the bad—I thank the Lord for the way he has directed my path. And it is clear to me now that Baba's untimely death was an important part of my journey. Although he was snatched from me when I was only six years old, he had already planted some important seeds of God's truth in my heart. And I can testify that some of those seeds have borne fruit for many years, while others are just now starting to sprout.

Sometimes it makes me sad to think that Baba left our family with almost nothing—nothing, that is, in worldly terms. He didn't own any property, and he left Mama with no resources to care for their six dear children. All we have are warm memories of a loving father who taught us to love each other, to love those around us, and most important of all, to love God above everything else. And when I really stop to think about it, I don't believe Baba could have given us anything better.

I do have one treasured keepsake from Baba, though, and I have held on to it ever since that terrible day he died all those years ago. That day, as we stood in front of the church with Ibrahim and Youssef, I didn't care about the hot sun or the dust clouds stirred up by the desert breeze. I just knew I was with my Baba, and nothing else mattered. That was all swept away when those two terrorists swooped down our narrow street and shot my father.

As Baba started to fall that day, I reached out to him but all I could grab was his old walking staff. There I stood beside my bleeding Baba, waiting for the ambulance to come, and for the next two hours I clung to that staff as if I were holding on to Baba himself.

When the ambulance drove away and Ibrahim took me inside, I took that walking staff with me, and I was still holding it on Sunday when Mama came home. That's when I decided nothing and no one would ever take it away from me. It was the only thing of Baba's I had left, and I still have it today.

Over the years Baba's staff has become a symbol of the goodness and grace of God to me, but it means so much more than that. It is a vivid reminder of the path Baba began walking back in Shotb and those other obscure places. I remember the way he would let me tag along like his little shadow, until his journey was suddenly cut short with so much left undone. And I am thankful every day that our loving Lord, in the perfect plan he designed for me before time began, is allowing me to complete Baba's journey.

It is easy sometimes to think we are the first ones who have ever walked through some dark valley of sorrow; but generally speaking, this is really not the case. Often we can find a person in the Bible who has experienced something similar. In my case there is a man from the Old Testament whose story is somewhat like mine—but much worse, to be sure. It is interesting to remember that he was also a dreamer, and that he once lived in Egypt too.

The book of Genesis tells us about Joseph, who suffered many painful things in his life. No doubt there were days when he thought God had forgotten him, when he wondered why he had to suffer so. And Joseph's story has helped me put the pieces of my puzzle together, especially when I get to verse 23 of Genesis 50. I have even changed the wording of the verse a bit to describe what happened that Friday in Karya Maghola. My version goes something like this: what the terrorists meant for evil, God intended for good. And with that Scripture in mind, I just continue the journey the Lord has laid out for me, knowing that his ways are the best ways no matter where they may take me.

So now you have heard my story . . . the story of how a little boy became a man, and how a loving God reshaped his young life from one filled with hatred and anger to a life filled and controlled by the love of Jesus. And the last chapters of my story have not even been written. I have no idea what they will say. But I know Someone who does, and I know I can trust him to help me write them.

Again, let me say that I don't want to claim any credit for the things you have read here. They are simply an example of what God will do for anyone—including you—who will invite the Lord Jesus to come and live in their heart.

And there is one final truth that I believe today more than ever: God's only Son Jesus is the answer for everything we face—both for today and for all of our tomorrows. He will always be the answer . . .

for you . . .

and for me . . .

and for our entire world!

Brother Nathan

ACKNOWLEDGMENTS

The book you now hold would never have been written without the help and input of many people. First and foremost is my dear friend Rody Rodeheaver, who has shared everything in my life, especially the events of these recent troubling times. Then I must thank Brian Vos for catching the spirit of my story and insisting that it should be told to a wider audience. I am very pleased that Baker Publishing Group agreed to make the book a reality. Special thanks for all of the helpful editorial insight and guidance Brian and the rest of the staff at Baker have provided. Finally I want to thank my friend David Culross, who took my story and shaped it in such a way that those who read these words can see, smell, touch, and feel these events that have forever altered my life. My prayer is that my story will alter your life, too, as you listen for God's voice in these pages.